Managing Publicly

Henry Mintzberg
Jacques Bourgault

Contributors:
Mohamed Charih
Martine Éthier
Jennifer Smith
Paul G. Thomas
David Zussman

Monographs on Canadian Public Administration – No. 25
Monographies sur l'administration publique canadienne – No. 25

Canadian Cataloguing in Publication Data

Mintzberg, Henry, 1939–
Managing publicly

(Monographs on Canadian public administration ; no. 25 = Monographies sur l'administration publique canadienne ; no. 25)
Issued also in French under title: Manager en public.
Co-published by Canadian Centre for Management Development.
ISBN 0-920715-98-2

1. Public administration. I. Bourgault, Jacques, 1945– .
II. Canadian Centre for Management Development.
III. Institute of Public Administration of Canada. IV. Title.
V. Series: Monographs on Canadian public administration ; no. 25.

JF1351.M56 2000 351 C00-932746-0

PUBLISHED BY / PUBLIÉ PAR

L'INSTITUT D'ADMINISTRATION PUBLIQUE DU CANADA
THE INSTITUTE OF PUBLIC ADMINISTRATION OF CANADA
1075, rue Bay St., Suite/Bureau 401
Toronto, Ontario, CANADA M5S 2B1
Tel./Tél.: (416) 924-8787 Fax/Bél.: (416) 924-4992
e-mail/courriel: ntl@ipaciapc.ca

Table of Contents

Foreword

Since the very earliest studies of public administration, scholars and practitioners have asked themselves what made managing in government different from managing in the private sector. The answers have varied with the ages.

It has long been appreciated that while many of the routine practices are similar in both government and in business, the missions and the mandates of the public and private sectors have often been seen as very different. Over the past generation, however, governments around the world have insisted that their operations be inspired by private-sector practices. In this vein, they have adopted a wider range of public-service delivery mechanisms, they have forged more partnerships with the private sector and community organizations, and have streamlined their operations. Indeed, government operations have changed so much that the question had to be asked once again: is government management different from private-sector management? What makes them similar, and what makes them distinctive? What are the implications of this new reality for management in the public sector?

Henry Mintzberg and Jacques Bourgault are eminently qualified to help us respond to these vital questions. Mintzberg conducted field studies and then forged his findings into a provocative model. Jacques Bourgault turned to practitioners in a roundtable for their views on what makes "managing publicly" so complex, and so very interesting, and then led a team of theorists to test the model.

The Institute of Public Administration of Canada and the Canadian Centre for Management Development are proud to support this vital conversation on the particular challenges of executives and managers in public administration at all levels of government. Managing publicly is a difficult task. It involves the performance of intricate tasks, the integration of differing views, the demands of rigorous policy work that takes into account short- and long-term objectives and the careful scrutiny of cabinet, Parliament and, ultimately, the people.

It is clear that the role of public-sector managers is being transformed. Like an orchestra's conductor, the job insists on communication, action and decision. The notion that government departments work in distinct "silos" (or as "soloists") is quickly being abandoned as senior managers respond to the need to integrate their work with each other on a variety of different issues.

We would like to thank the co-editors, Henry Mintzberg and Jacques Bourgault, the CCMD research group who sponsored the initial research and the roundtable, the academics and practitioners who attended the roundtable, the authors of the chapters, the IPAC research team which managed the publication process, and the many other people who made this book possible.

This volume adds novel insights, provocative models and sharp perspectives to our knowledge about this new reality, ones that will be discussed and argued over for many years to come. We may not all be able to agree on the distinctive nature of the challenges faced by government, but there is no doubt that the study of public administration has been strengthened by this important contribution.

Errol S. Price
President, Institute of Public Administration of Canada

Jocelyne Bourgon
President, Canadian Centre for Management Development

Acknowledgements

The authors would like to express their deepest appreciation to the Canadian Centre for Management Development, the École nationale d'administration publique, the Université du Québec à Montréal, the Institute of Public Administration of Canada and its Montreal regional group, and McGill University for their financial assistance and essential support during this long process, which included organizing seminars, research and publication of this book. They are particularly indebted to Pierre De Celles, Maurice Demers, Nicole Fontaine, Joe Galimberti, Ralph Heintzman, Geoff McIlroy, Patrice Dutil and Paul Pross.

We would like to thank the monograph series editors, Peter Aucoin and Vincent Lemieux, and the two anonymous reviewers who provided helpful suggestions. And special thanks to the eight public-sector managers who so graciously let Henry follow them for a day.

This book could not have been produced without the valuable help of Santa Balanca-Rodrigues, Pia Bruni, Chantal Carstens, Martine Éthier, Carole Garand, Ginette Guilbault, Élyse Labrecque, Élisabeth Laviolette, Christiane Miroglio, Laurence Viens-Huard, and all those involved in the translation, especially Professor Gladys L Symons – thank you all!

Managing in the Public Sector: Introduction and Overview[1]

Jacques Bourgault

Some thirty-three years ago, Henry Mintzberg made his first observations of time management and managerial roles in the private sector. Today, the public sector is in the process of transforming its management strategies to resemble those of the private sector. In this context, the questions we ask are the following: How do senior and middle managers in the pubic sector perceive their role? How do their time management strategies reflect this perception?

Some simply state that "managing is managing" regardless of sector and that to manage well in the public sector is no different from managing well in the private sector. Moreover, the two sectors are drawn ever closer together, whether by imitation, partnership or complementarity. Others contend that real organizational conditions (e.g., problem complexity, finances, mandate limits, unionization rate, rigidity, need for transparency, multiple controls, limited legal capacity, monopoly), the environment (proximity to politics, numerous contradictory pressures, citizen expectations, plurality of partners and stakeholders), and organizational goals (the public interest, the obligation to achieve the goals of the law regardless of cost) are so different that the performance expected of managers in the public sector will vary from that in the private sector. The wise decisions and attitudes of private-sector managers would be catastrophic (or at least a time bomb!) in the public domain.

Innumerable attempts to differentiate between the public and private sectors have been proposed, including a recent one by Richard C. Box.[2] On the one hand, Box attributes to private-sector CEOs a large measure of managerial autonomy, a personal vision for the future, the right to secrecy, and the capacity and skills for risk-taking. They work with a coercion–domination model, have the right to proceed with drastic, sudden and rapid change, and experience the peculiarity of evolving in a milieu that feels no obligation to respect tradition. By contrast, public-sector managers operate in a context of multiple accountabilities, and, when establishing a vision for the future, they must take into consideration the participation of many others (including politicians, groups and citizens). They manage in a showcase, elaborate policies in a process exposed to public scrutiny, and must direct and guide rather than dominate. Imbued with community values, public managers are obliged in their entrepreneurship to take into account the impact of their actions on public processes and products in terms of appropriateness, adequacy, justice, representation and participation.

The minister responsible for the State Services Commission of the Government of New Zealand, Paul East, has identified the principal values of public-sector managers: ethical conduct, obedience, loyalty, neutrality, a sense of the public good, equity, and the desire for professional and technical excellence.[3] Their counterparts in the private sector, by contrast, have an instinct for productivity (e.g., system efficiency, high production standards, product quality, preoccupation with costs and delays). The private-sector manager is attentive to client needs, excels at assessing trends, adapts rapidly, and is able to make painful decisions. East criticizes the cannibalism of private-sector management, with its tendency to overspend on advertising and senior management pay-packages. He deplores public-sector managers' fears of change, real delegation, technological innovations, and competition, as well as their sense of immortality.

Both sectors embrace similar management functions, but the context and constraints of each sector affect the managerial role and the way it is performed. The relationship between the elements of the managerial role consequently varies, as do the attitudes of the managers in each milieu. These differences must be taken into account for recruitment, education and training. To a certain extent, the relative convergence of management practices in these sectors reduces the difference in performance of the managerial functions and the performance of managerial roles. In the final analysis, the remaining distinguishing features will win out over the converging ones: managers in the private sector will always be asked questions like, "What did you do for my stocks today?", while their counterparts in the public sector will be asked, "Have you applied the law well? as well as possible? in the interest of the users? the beneficiaries? the citizens? the state? as efficiently as possible?

Following the example of many others, Leonard White, Henri Fayol, Bernard Gournay, Georges Langrod, and Peter Blau have contributed to the recognition of the concept of *public administration / administration publique* by applying one of the following concepts: 1) the set of organizations, laws and employees intended to set up and manage the social contract; 2) the pursuit of these social goals through a variety of more or less active and direct state interventions; 3) public administration as the discipline of teaching and research, dedicated to integrating other disciplines used to support the action of the state (e.g., law, economics, sociology, social psychology, management, political science) and also dedicated to professional practice.[4]

For the sake of argument, we shall include in our conception / definition of public administration *public* organisms – directors of public property centrally controlled by the minister and government secretariat at the political level, by central agencies (Treasury Board, Public Service Commission) at the resource level, and subject to direct control by Parliament. We shall also include the *parapublic* sector – bodies (state-owned companies, councils, quasi-ministries and quasi-judicial bodies) and the three networks of education, municipal management, and health and social services that are indirectly subject to the same controls. We exclude the *peripublic* sector – private bodies (whether for-profit or not-for-profit) that produce goods of public interest that are in some way seen to be essential for society (e.g., professional corporations, certain communications and resource firms controlled by regulations and quasi-judicial bodies). In the absence of positive law, in a country like Canada, which has no real system of administrative law, there are no such *appellations controlées* in these matters. The boundaries between the public and parapublic sectors are inconsistent. In the dozen or so public acts aimed at establishing these boundaries, the boundaries are specific to the intentions of the act. This distinction between sectors may seem very semantic. That the distinction is based on the notion of autonomy of organizational units with respect to central power affects the intellectual and political leeway available to managers to establish the "job frame" and the performance of roles directed towards information, people and action. This is made clear in Mintzberg's model.

Simplifying the matter, if management *were* management, we should expect to see managers performing the same roles regardless of rank. The only things that would change would be the *scope* of the role, the level of one's respondents and the level of conglomeration, or the level of complexity of the issues. But one is not responsible for the total performance of the organization. Rather, one is in charge of a more specialized sector and of more operational objectives. At this level, one deals with interlocutors with fewer titles, and, in certain cases, one does so as a subordinate. At the top of the pyramid, however, managers must have a strategic vision. They are more likely to deal with the environment or with high-level colleagues, while internal transactions take place with subordinates.

With the development of a more technocratic approach in the 1940s[5], almost one hundred years after De Tocqueville, management as a concept was brought to the fore. But the concept really only began to penetrate the public-sector literature in the 1960s. The development of the science of management in that decade refined conceptual distinctions, such that more and more specialists deliberately articulate the particular sense and utility of each concept. Others confound management and administration through indifference or ignorance, while we now give a different meaning to these *appellations 'non-controlees.'*

Whereas the advocates of the synonym approach denounce the proliferation of "redundant concepts," more and more observers see this as a normal evolution of scientific knowledge. Administrative science appeared, was accepted, and immediately split into disciplines claiming even greater recognition. This pattern is, in fact, very common, as can be seen in the case of public administration. Fifty years ago, the social psychology of organizations did not exist as a domain of teaching and professional practice. Later, it found a place within management science and became an autonomous field. Fifty years ago, the École libre de science politique de Paris permitted the founding of the French École nationale d'administration (ÉNA). At that time, teaching political science was neither well developed nor highly respected in Quebec, and it was not until around 1960 that a department of political science emerged within the social sciences. Near the end of the 1960s, public administration was introduced into bachelor of arts programs, and many schools and departments of public administration emerged throughout Canada. Even at the beginning of the 1970s, management had still not found its niche, for the faculties of management in large universities were often called the Faculty of Commerce! Today, faculties of management are largely subdivided into specialities.

Alas, it seems that the terms "administration," "*gestion*," "management" and "commerce" are often thrown around and used willy-nilly, whether in titles of books, faculties or programs. There are, nonetheless, some fundamental differences in these terms. In public administration, the more legal continental European approaches differ from the more American managerial ones, both anglophone and francophone, as can be seen in the programs of consultation and international cooperation at the École nationale d'administration publique (ÉNAP) in Hull, Quebec.

Given the evolution of knowledge and disciplines, we should now reserve the term "administration" to designate an action that applies legal, statutory, political, and program norms to cases for decision. Such action is quite typical, frequent and repetitive, leaving little room for discretion. It is applied most often at the base of the hierarchy, even though the most senior civil servants engage in administrative actions when they apply policies or human resource management rules to their immediate subordinates (for example, a president to his or her vice-presidents). In fact, the higher one goes up the pyramid, the less time is accorded to administrative tasks, at least for those who keep within their sphere of performance.

In French, we could avoid confusion by reserving the term *gestion* for the job of middle and senior managers at all levels of the organization. This involves reaching objectives by the optimal deployment of the resources these managers control (e.g., legal authority, prestige, human, financial and material resources, the reputation of the organization), while respecting the constraints (e.g., legislation, labour agreements, norms, policies) imposed on them as givens. In English, the term "manager" refers to both the CEOs and the senior managers. Within the constraints imposed on them, senior managers must calculate and optimize resource utilization and goals.[6] Senior managers enjoy a degree of discretion that increases as they climb the organizational ladder. At the top of the pyramid, the preoccupation with optimizing becomes more "macro" and has more serious career consequences.

Finally, the term "manager" should be reserved for the most senior employees of an organization; the senior manager in charge of organizational creativity, imagining solutions and finding answers. In effect, the senior manager is the one who ensures that what needs to get done, gets done.[7] Four components of the managerial role are included in this definition. The manager sees to it that systems are put in place. He or she must anticipate what should be done. He or she must see that it gets done, and the manager will be evaluated, first of all, on the result, not just on the effort. The senior manager has a lot of room to manœuvre but little space for errors.

In fact, each manager in the pyramid fulfils the roles of manager, *gestionnaire* and administrator; however, within the specific performance zone of each, the proportion of time and effort expended changes, with the management dimension increasing near the top of the hierarchy. Deputy ministers (equivalent to CEOs) spend about seventy per cent of their time on the four components of management, twenty-five per cent optimizing the deployment of the organizational structure and the activity of their managers, and five per cent applying certain policies to their immediate subordinates. One can imagine radically different proportions at the base of the hierarchy: professionals or clerks administer policies and programs for about eighty-five per cent of their time, optimize the layout of their professional environment for about ten to twelve per cent, and spend the rest of the time making sure that whatever needs to be done (at their level) gets done.

In English, the problem is both simple and complex. It is simpler, because there is no specific term to translate *gestion* from the French. But it is consequently more complex, because the term "management" can have several quite different meanings.

Today, the term *administration* (when not referring to the entire American federal bureaucracy) appears to mean the organization and application of a law, a policy or a procedure, as it does in French. In English, the term "management" seems to refer to an intellectual discipline (as does the term "administration"), but it also designates the two most senior types of leaders. Management refers to CEOs (chief executive officers) and CAOs (chief administrative officers), but it also designates middle managers as well as foremen, even including those who manage parking lots and bowling alleys!

Going beyond a strictly terminological approach, it is important to visualize what the challenges are, as well as the contribution to organizational performance at each hierarchical level, as Pierre Jeanniot, now president of the International Air Transport Association (IATA), brilliantly demonstrated.[8] At the top, the senior manager must identify, make, and take responsibility for, decisions, especially strategic ones, and see that they are carried out. In the middle of the pyramid, the manager must make and participate in tactical decisions to optimize resources to achieve the objectives assigned to each level, given the constraints. At the lower level of the pyramid, the manager must carry out policies in the everyday operations of production, delivery and support, hence the term "operational decisions."

What, then, are the roles of the manager and how can we apply them to the public-sector reality at the beginning of a new millennium? These are the questions this volume will try to address.

MANAGERIAL ROLES IN THE PUBLIC SECTOR: THE GENESIS OF THIS BOOK

The genesis of this book has come from a variety of successive managerial initiatives. In 1993, Professor Henry Mintzberg spent some time observing how middle managers from different backgrounds and various ranks organized their time. Three series of observations were planned. From the spring to the autumn of that year, Mintzberg travelled to Alberta, Nova Scotia and Ottawa to observe public managers in three sites: Parks Canada, the Royal Canadian Mounted Police, and the federal Department of Justice. He wanted to contextualize his observations by first developing a model of the roles he observed for middle managers. The chapters in Part One of this book present the details of his observations and how the roles and aspects of managerial work in the public sector can be synthesized into an integrative model.

Mintzberg shows how the manager develops a "job frame," which is the central point of a series of concentric circles of roles. These roles include focusing on *information* (communicating and controlling), on *people* (managing in the sense of being a leader and linking people), and on *action* (doing the job himself or herself and negotiating or encouraging others). These roles are performed according to the character or the style of each manager.

The case of Parks Canada illustrates the richness of the situations found "on the edges" (Chapter 2) between users, interest groups, managers (both in the periphery and at the centre), and politicians. Mintzberg presents a typology of the "job frame": sharp or vague; imposed or selected by the manager. Here he depicts the crucial nature of the role of the interface between managerial type and interest groups – management directed outward and management directed towards the base of the pyramid.

The case of the Royal Canadian Mounted Police, in Chapter 3, demonstrates the use of culture in organizational control, which produces a more traditional, subliminal and, therefore, a less conflictual form of social control. Mintzberg depicts an organizational form "tri-dimensionally" designed to be controlled more from the "centre," by a rigorously programmed central core, than from the top. This form of "normative" control differs from other forms observed in governmental systems, such as the government-as-machine model, the network model, the performance-control model, the virtual-government model and the normative-control model.

In the Department of Justice, Mintzberg observed a place where the conception of a large set of government policies exists alongside the administration of many of those policies, as well as the administration of programs and resources of the department (Chapter 4). Is implementing policies part of management? Indeed, it is, for the government is a social venture, and, like all ventures, it needs guidelines. How can one bring together the different functions of adviser and manager at the top? How can one bring together administrative units with such different mandates under the same structure? Mintzberg proposes an approach of managing by conglomerate.

Part Two of this book presents several contributions that discuss the cases and analyse Mintzberg's integrative model. The first of these discussions took place as a roundtable, excerpts of which are in Chapter 5. On 26 February 1998, at the Sheraton Hotel in Montreal, senior managers from the public sector and academics from universities and research institutes were invited to a seminar organized by the Montreal Regional

Group of the Institute of Public Administration of Canada. Professor Mintzberg began this seminar by giving a forty-five-minute presentation to an audience of over 250 people. Using his presentation as a point of departure, the participants in this roundtable discussion gathered to share their common experiences. (Some time before this event, the participants had received from Mintzberg a hundred-page document outlining his observations and model.) The roundtable lasted three hours, and, had it not been for the very busy schedules of all concerned, the seminar would have continued for many more days. The discussions were tape-recorded, and the participants were invited to contribute to the present volume. In these texts, the reader will find three debates: a comparison of public and private management; a discussion of roles played by different levels of management; and a model depicting and integrating public managerial roles.

We then present four commentaries of prospective and empirical studies from professors of political science, management and public administration. David Zussman and Jennifer Smith examine in Chapter 6 the socio-professional characteristics of Canadian deputy ministers, and their counterparts in the private sector, and analyse the impact of the similarities and differences of their role performance. In Chapter 7, Mohamed Charih comments on Mintzberg's model as a whole and then examines each of its developments in turn. Paul G. Thomas, in Chapter 8, considers the impact of new public management and citizen expectations (especially those from political circles) on the role choices of public managers. In Chapter 9, I test Mintzberg's conclusions with his studies on productivity and time management of federal deputy ministers and with his studies on the satisfaction of federal ministers with respect to deputy ministers' performance of the functions and attributes of their job.

In this book, we have made use of three different approaches: inductive and deductive analysis; empirical research; and the structured accounts of actors. We hope to achieve the following goals: 1) identify to what extent "managing is managing," regardless of the circumstances; 2) underscore the specificity of certain components of the managerial role in the public sector; and 3) depict the specific context of public management as the two sectors move towards convergence.

More than ever, public management is in the forefront, as we scrutinize more closely the productivity and efficiency of public organizations. Senior managers face more challenges in these changing times. Observing their work, as well as listening to their stories, is of particular interest now that they are at the crossroads. Managers are required to manage more and more like their private-sector counterparts, while respecting the traditional values of the public sector. Politicians, citizens and the media judge their performance daily. Societal complexity, the rate and extent of social change, and fiscal pressures have raised expectations with respect to how well public managers perform their roles. Globalization makes the roles of public managers even more important, all other factors being equal. It will be the integrity of public policy, ethical conduct and efficiency of public-service delivery that will provide a competitive field and that will attract and maintain investments and the skills that contribute to national wealth. We hope this volume will go some way in illuminating what it is to manage publicly.

NOTES

1 I am grateful to Gladys L. Symons, professor, École nationale d'administration publique, for translating this chapter.
2 Richard C. Box, "Running government like a business: implications for public administration and practice," *American Review of Public Administration* 29, no. 1 (March 1999), pp. 19–43.
3 Paul East, "Notes for Remarks to the New Zealand Institute for Public Administration," October 1994.
4 Leonard White, *Introduction to the Study of Public Administration*, 4th edition (New York: Macmillan, 1955); Henri Fayol, *Administration industrielle et générale*, new edition (Paris: Dunod, 1999); Bernard Gournay, *Introduction à l'administration publique* (Paris: Presses de la Fondation nationales des sciences politiques, 1968); Georges Langrod, *Traité des Sciences administratives* (Paris: Mouton, 1966); Peter Blau, *The Dynamics of Bureaucracy* (Chicago: Chicago University Press, 1963).
5 James Burnham, *The Managerial Revolution: What is Happening in the World*, revised edition (Westport, Conn.: Greenwood Press, 1972).
6 Jacques Lebraty, "Management et gestion : quel apprentissage?" *Economies et sociétés* 26, no. 7 (1992).
7 Ibid.
8 Pierre Jeanniot and Jacques Bourgault, "Le processus décisionnel dans le secteur public: le cas d'Air Canada," *Gestion* 3, no. 2, (April 1978), pp. 52–63.

PART ONE

Developing a Model for Managing Publicly

Henry Mintzberg

1

Managing

Managing may be managing, but the public sector is not the private sector. A model of managerial work may apply appropriately to both, but only as long as the differences are made clear.

Of course, the differences within each of these sectors can be as vast as the differences between them. Just as managing a corner grocery store is hardly the same as managing Power Corporation, so managing a national park is hardly the same as managing the federal Department of Justice. Government is life, in some sense, and is almost as varied as life itself, since it touches almost every aspect of life.

Part One of this book will attempt to capture some of the flavour and variety of managing in the public sector. The following chapters in this section are based on the observation of a day in the life of eight federal managers; three in the Western Region of Parks Canada, three in the Royal Canadian Mounted Police, and two in the Department of Justice. These observations are part of a larger study of managerial work that has involved twenty-nine managers in all. This work was supported by the Canadian Centre for Management Development (CCMD), which kindly covered the costs of transportation and lodging associated with these eight days.

One day is not a long time and may not be representative of the nature of a person's job. The sample of eight days, however, does begin to develop a sense of what it is like to manage in different spheres of today's government.

A MODEL OF MANAGERIAL WORK

This research was designed to elaborate and enhance a model of managerial work, especially that concerning the "what" and "how" of the job.

Figure 1.1 *The Person in the Job*

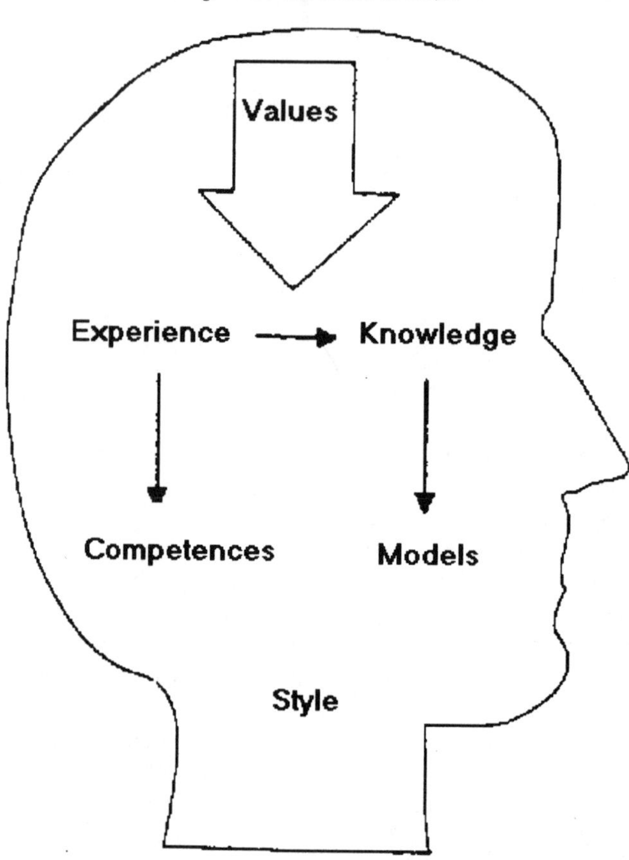

What roles or aspects of the job of managing do particular managers tend to favour, and how do they carry out these roles? Such description is meant to provide a richer understanding of different styles of managing.[1]

In 1973, I published *The Nature of Managerial Work*, one chapter of which specified the roles that all managers seem to carry out. I was dissatisfied with this book for a number of reasons, including the fact that, like almost all other descriptions of managerial work, it constituted a decomposed list rather than an interactive model.[2] A new framework, closer in form to a model, was developed, based on a review and integration of the various roles described in the literature of managerial work.

The model is made up of concentric circles (see Figure 1.1). At the centre sits the person who brings to the job a set of values, experiences, knowledge, mental models and competences. The person in the job creates a

Figure 1.2 *The "Frame" in the Job*

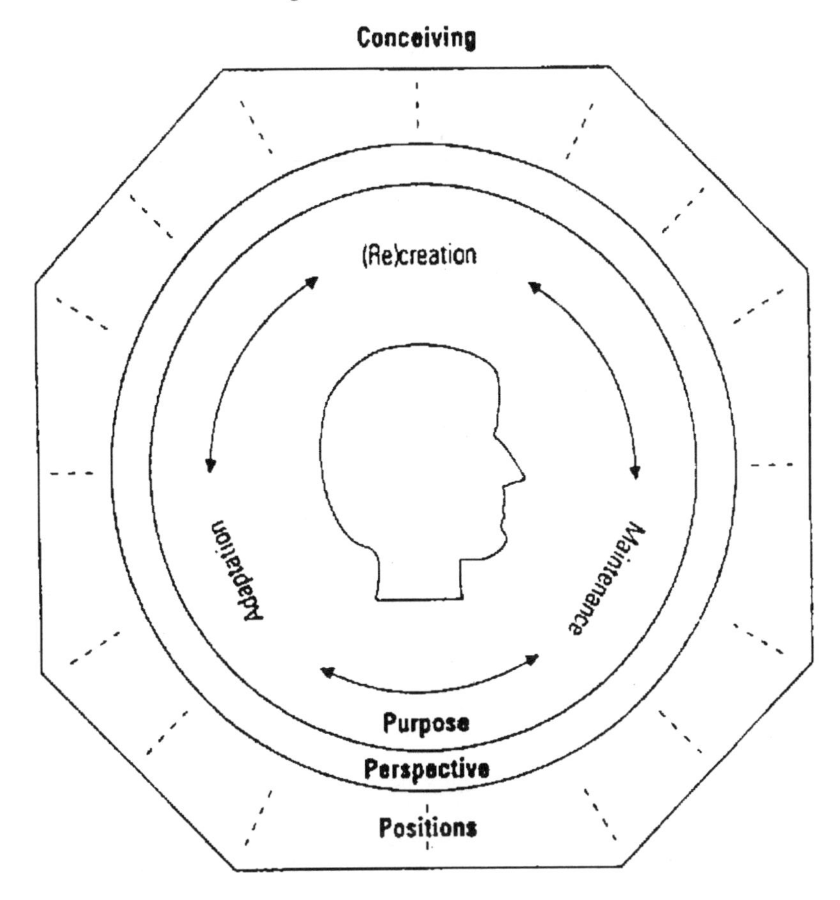

"frame" (shown in Figure 1.2). The frame includes 1) the purpose of the job, namely what is to be accomplished over some period of time, 2) a perspective on what needs to be done, in the sense of an overall strategic vision or worldview – which can range from creating or recreating something new, through adapting what is currently in place, to maintaining the status quo – and 3) specific positions for doing it, meaning some tangible strategies, such as a reorganization or the introduction of some particular new services, for bringing the perspective to life. This frame can range from being rather vague to highly specific and from being self-selected by the manager to being imposed externally. The frame is in turn manifested by an agenda of specific issues and work schedules (Figure 1.3).

All of this can be thought to constitute the basic core of the job of man-

Figure 1.3 *The Agenda of the Job*

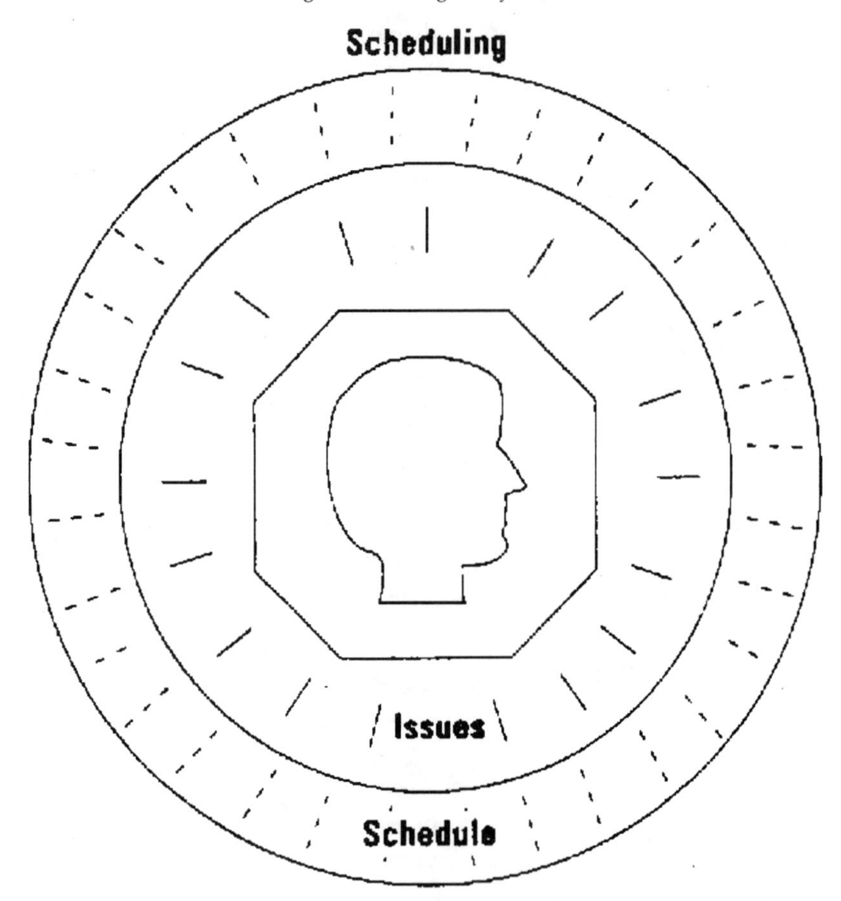

aging. It sits, as shown in Figure 1.4, between the unit being managed (referred to as "inside") and what is outside that (whether within the rest of the organization), to the world at large.

Surrounding the core are three concentric circles that represent three levels (information, people and action) through which managerial work can take place (Figure 1.5). From the centre, beginning with the most abstract level, a manager can process information in the hope that this will drive people to take action. More tangibly, a manager can work with people to encourage them to take action. And at the most concrete level, a manager can manage action more or less directly. Figure 1.6 shows the full model. In addition to the roles of conceiving the frame and scheduling the agenda, indicated within the core, six roles are shown in the outer

Figure 1.4 *The Core in Context*

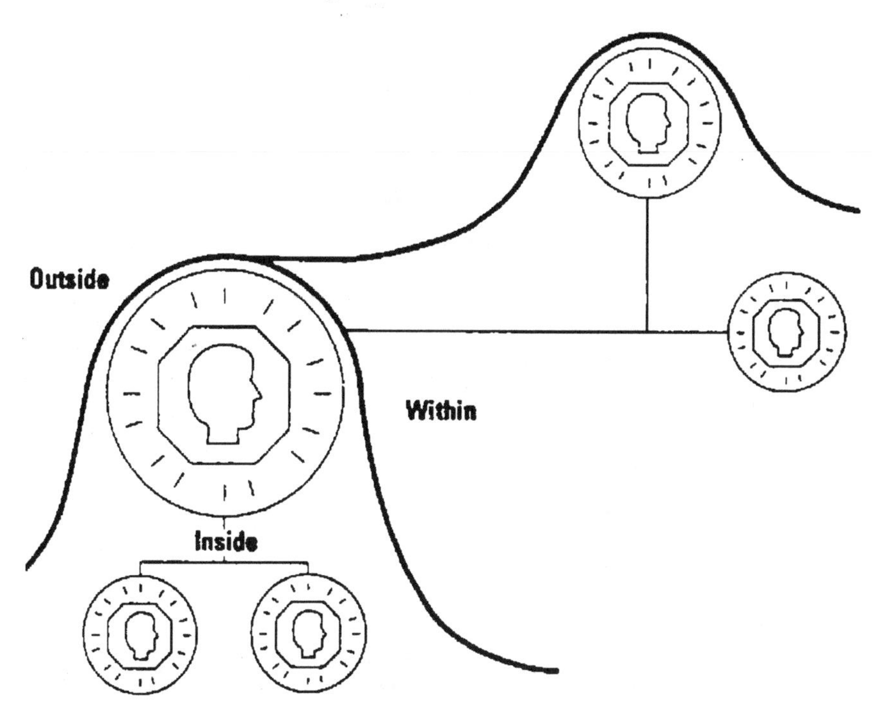

circles, two at the information level, two at the people level, and two at the action levels. These are described below.

Managing by Information

To manage by information is to be two steps removed from the ultimate purpose of managerial work. The manager processes information to drive other people who, in turn, are supposed to ensure that the necessary actions are taken. In other words, here the manager's own activities focus neither on people nor on action per se but rather on information as an indirect way of making things happen. Ironically, while this was the classic description of managerial work for the first half of the twentieth century, in recent years it has become newly popular – in some quarters an almost obsessional view, epitomized by the so-called bottom-line approach to management.

Communication refers to the collection and dissemination of information. Managers devote a great deal of effort to the two-way flow of infor-

Figure 1.5 *Three Levels of Evoking Action*

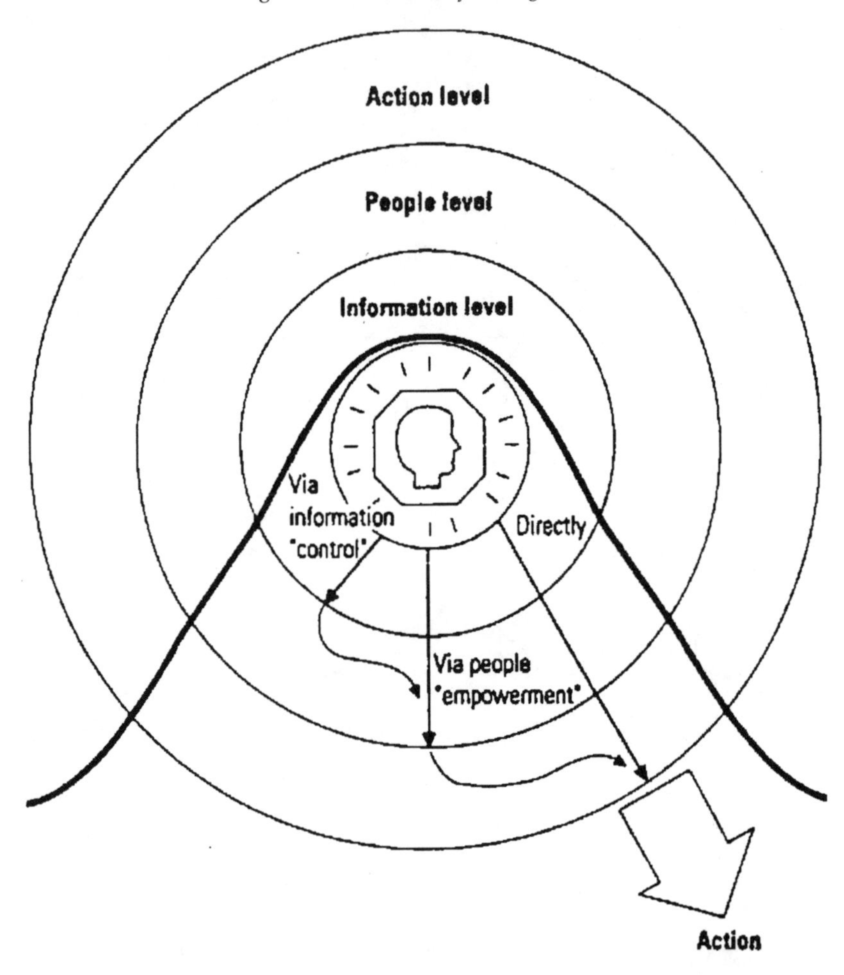

mation with the people all around them: the employees inside their own units, others in the rest of the organization, and, especially, as the empirical evidence makes abundantly clear, a great number of outsiders with whom they maintain regular contact.

Managers "scan" their environments, they monitor their own units, and they share with, and disseminate to, others considerable amounts of the information they acquire. A point worth emphasizing, and one emphasized in almost every serious study of managerial work, is that the formal information – in other words, information capable of being processed in a computer – does not play a particular dominant role here. Oral information, much of it too early or too "soft" to formalize – gossip, hearsay and even non-verbal information, namely what is seen and "felt" but not heard – forms a critical part of every serious managerial job or, at least, every managerial job performed seriously.

In my initial study, I described managers as "nerve centres" of their units who use their status of office to gain access to a wide variety of informational sources. Inside the unit, everyone else is a specialist who generally knows more about his or her speciality than does the manager. But, because the manager is connected to all those specialists, he or she should have the broadest base of knowledge about the unit in general. And, externally, by virtue of their status, managers have access to other managers who are themselves nerve centres of their own units. And so they tend to be exposed to powerful sources of external information and thus emerge as external nerve centres as well.

The result of all this is that a considerable amount of the manager's information turns out to be privileged, especially when we consider how much of it is oral and non-verbal. Accordingly, to function effectively with the people around them, managers have to spend considerable time sharing their information, both with outsiders, in a kind of spokesperson role, and with insiders, in a kind of disseminator role.

I found in my initial study of chief executives that perhaps forty per cent of their time was devoted almost exclusively to the *communicating* role – just to gain and share information – leaving aside the information processing aspects of all the other roles. In other words, the job of managing is fundamentally one of processing information, notably by talking and especially listening. Thus, Figure 1.6 shows the inner core (the person in the job, conceiving and scheduling) connected to the outer rings (the more tangible roles of managing people and action) through what can be called the membrane of information-processing all around the job.

What can be called the *controlling* role describes the managers' efforts to use information in a directive way inside their units: to evoke or provoke general action in the people who report to them. Managers do this in three broad ways: they develop systems, they design structures, and they impose directives. Each of these seeks to control how other people work, especially with regard to the allocation of resources, and what actions they are inclined to take.

First, developing systems is the most general of these three and the closest to conceiving. It uses information to control people's behaviour. Managers often take charge of establishing and even running such systems in their units, including systems of planning and performance-control, such as budgeting. Robert Simons has noted how chief executives

Figure 1.6 *A Model of Managerial Work*

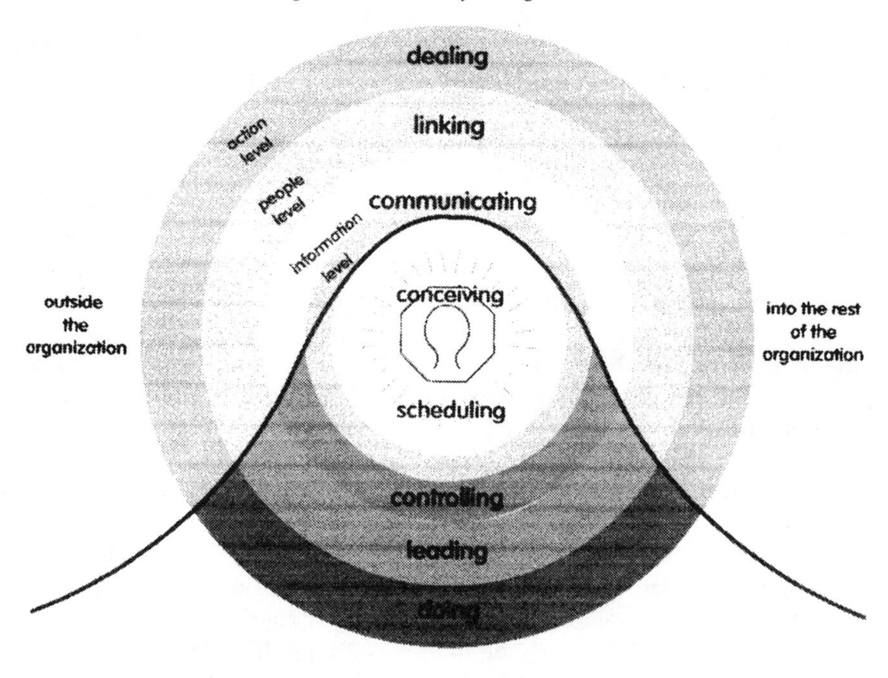

tend to select one such system and make it key to their exercise of control, in a manner he calls "interactive."[3]

Second, managers exercise control through designing the structures of their units. By establishing responsibilities and defining hierarchical authority, they actively, rather than passively, exercise control through the processing of information. People are informed of their duties, and this in turn is expected to drive them to carry out the appropriate actions.

A third way to control how people work is to impose directives, which is the most direct of the three, closest to the people and the action, although still informational in nature. Managers pronounce. They make specific choices and give specific orders, usually in the process of "delegating" particular responsibilities and "authorizing" particular requests. In effect, managers manage by transmitting information to people so that they can act.

If a full decision-making process can be considered in the three stages of diagnosing – designing, and deciding, in other words, identifying issues, working out possible solutions, and selecting one[4] – then here we are dealing with a restricted view of decision-making. Delegating means mostly diagnosing ("Would you please handle this problem in this context?"), while authorizing means mostly deciding ("OK, you can proceed."). Either way, the richest part of the process, the stage of designing possible solutions, resides with the person being controlled rather than with the manager, whose own behaviour remains rather passive. Thus, the manger as controller seems less an actor with sleeves rolled up, digging in, than a reviewer who sits back in the office and passes judgement. That is why this role is characterized as informational; a richer approach to decision-making is described under the *action* roles.

The *controlling* role is shown in Figure 1.6 propelling down into the manager's own unit, since that is where formal authority is exercised. The proximity of the controlling role to the manager's agenda reflects the fact that informational control is the most direct way to operationalize the agenda – for example, by using budgets to impose priorities or delegation to assign responsibilities.

The controlling role is, of course, what people have in mind when they refer to the "administrative" aspect of managerial work. Interestingly, it encompasses almost the entire set of activities described by the classical writers. In the 1930s, for example, Luther Gulick and Lyndall F. Urwick popularized the acronym POSDCORB (planning, organizing, staffing, directing, coordinating, reporting and budgeting).[5] Planning, organizing, directing and budgeting are all clearly focused here, while reporting, coordinating and staffing (in the sense of deciding) have important, although not exclusive, controlling aspects. Thus, it must be concluded that the long, popular description of managerial work was not so much wrong as narrow, focusing almost exclusively on one restricted aspect of the job: informational control of the unit through the exercise of formal authority.

Managing through People

To manage through people, instead of by information, is to move one step closer to action but still to remain removed from it. That is because here the focus of managerial attention becomes "affect" instead of "effect." Other people, not the manager him- or herself, or even necessarily the substance of the manager's thoughts, become the means to get things done.

After several decades of POSDCORB thinking and Taylorist technique, the Hawthorne experiments of the 1930s demonstrated with dramatic impact that management has to do with more than just the passive informational control of subordinates.[6] People entered the scene, or at least they entered the textbooks, as entities to be "motivated" and, later, "empowered." Influencing began to replace informing, and commitment began to vie with calculation for the attention of the manager.

The leading role has probably received more attention in the literature of management than have all the other roles combined. And so we need not dwell on it here. But neither can we ignore it: managers certainly do much more than lead the people in their own units. And leading certainly infuses much else of what managers do – as, in fact, do all the roles, as we have already noted about communicating. But their work just as certainly cannot be understood without this dimension. We can describe the role of leading on three levels.

First, managers lead on the individual level, "one on one," as the expression goes. They encourage and drive the people of their units: they motivate them, inspire them, coach them, nurture them, push them, mentor them, and so on. Second, managers lead on the group level, especially by building and managing teams, an activity that has received considerable attention in recent years. And, third, managers lead on the unit level, especially with regard to the creation and maintenance of culture, another subject of increasing attention in recent years, thanks especially to the Japanese. Managers, for example, engage in many acts of a symbolic nature ("figurehead" duties) to sustain culture.

All managers seem to spend time on all three levels of leadership, although, again, styles do vary according to context and personality. If the communicating role describes the manager as the nerve centre of the unit, then the leading role must characterize him or her as its "energy centre," a concept perhaps best captured in M. Maeterlinck's wonderful description of the "spirit of the hive."[7] Given the right managerial "chemistry" – in the case of Maeterlinck's queen bee, quite literally – it may be the manager's mere presence that somehow draws things together. By exuding that mystical substance, the leader unites his or her people, galvanizing them into action to accomplish the unit's mission and adapt it to a changing world.

The excess attention to the role of leading has probably been matched by the inadequate attention to the role of linking. For in their sheer allocation of time, managers have been shown to be external linkers as much as they are internal leaders. In 1964, Leonard Sayles emphasized this in his path-breaking book, and I repeated it in my 1973 book, as did John Kotter in his of 1982.[8] Yet, the point hardly seems appreciated. Indeed, now more than ever, this role must be understood, given the great growth of alliances, joint ventures, and other collaborating and networking relationships between organizations, as well as the gradual reconception of the "captive" employee as an autonomous "agent" who supplies labour.

The manager is both an advocate of the unit's influence outside of it and, in turn, a recipient of much of the influence exerted on it from the outside. But he or she must regulate the receipt of external influence to protect the unit – to use a popular term, be a "gatekeeper" of influence. Or, to add a metaphor, the manager acts as a kind of valve between the unit and its environment.

All managers, as emphasized in other research and my studies cited earlier, appear to spend a great deal of time "networking," which means building vast arrays of contacts and intricate coalitions of supporters beyond their own units, whether within the rest of the organization or outside, in the world at large. To all these contacts, the manager represents the unit externally, promotes its needs, and lobbies for its causes. In response, these people are expected to provide a steady inflow of information to the unit, as well as various means of support and specific favours for it.

In turn, people intent on influencing the behaviour of an organization or one of its sub-units will often exercise pressure directly on its managers, expecting that person to transmit the influence inside. Here, then, the managerial job becomes one of delicate balance, a tricky act of mediation. Those managers who let external influence pass inside too freely, acting like sieves, are apt to drive their people crazy. Of course, those who act like sponges and absorb all the influence personally are apt to drive themselves crazy! And those who block out all influence, acting like lead to X-rays, are apt to detach their units from reality and so dry up the sources of external support. Thus, the choice of what influence to pass on and how, bearing in mind the quid pro quo that influence exerted out is likely to be mirrored by influence coming back in, becomes another key aspect of managerial style, worthy of greatly increased attention in both the study of the job and the training of its occupants.

Managing Action

If managers manage passively by information and effectively through people, then they also manage actively and instrumentally by their own direct involvement in action. Indeed, this has been a long-established view of managerial work, although the excess attention in the twentieth century, first to controlling and then to leading, and more recently to conceiving of deliberate strategy, has obscured its importance. Leonard Sayles, however, has long and steadily insisted on this, beginning with his 1964 book and culminating in *The Working Leader* (1993), in which he made his strongest statement yet, insisting that managers must be the focal points for action in and by their units.[9] Their direct involvement must, in his view, take precedence over the pulling force of leadership and the pushing force of controllership.

Doing is a popular label in the managerial vernacular ("Mary Ann's a doer!"). But it is necessary to point out that managers, in fact, hardly ever "do" anything. Some don't even enter their own telephones numbers! As already noted, watch a manager and you will see someone whose work consists almost exclusively of talking and listening, alongside, of course, of watching and "feeling." That, incidentally, is why the manager is shown at the core of the model as a head and not as a full body!

What "doing" presumably means, therefore, is getting closer to the action, ultimately being just one step removed from it. Managers as doers manage the carrying out of action directly, instead of indirectly, by managing people or by processing information. In effect, a "doer" is really someone who gets it done or, as the French put it with their expression, *fait faire,* to "make something get made." And the managerial vernacular is, in fact, full of expressions that reflect just this: "championing change," "fighting fires," "juggling projects," etc. In the terms of decision-making introduced earlier, here the manager diagnoses and designs as well as decides: he or she gets deeply and fully involved in the management of particular activities.

Doing involves projects and problems inside the unit. This does not imply that projects are independent of problems or that either are exclusively internal. Rather, it means that much "doing" has to do with changing the unit itself, both proactively and reactively. Managers champion change to exploit opportunities for their units, and they handle its problems and resolve its crises, often with "hands-on" involvement.

The difference between deciding in the controlling role and acting in the doing role is the difference, in effect, between sitting in a managerial office and passing judgement on the issues floating by – "Roberta, please handle this." "No, Joe, you can't do that." – and getting out of the office and actively engaging issues from their initial identification to their final resolution. Here the manager becomes a true designer, not of abstract strategies or of generalized structures, but of tangible projects of change. And the evidence, in fact, is that managers at all levels typically juggle many such projects concurrently, perhaps several dozen in the case of the chief executives. Hence the popularity of the term "project management."

Managers "do" in two other respects as well. For one thing, they sometimes do the routine work of their units in the place of other people. Of course, when managers are replacing absent employees, this may be considered another aspect of handling problems. Second, some managers continue to do regular work after they have become managers. The Pope leads prayers and a dean might teach a class. Done for its own sake, this might be considered separate from managerial work. But such things are often done for very managerial reasons as well. This may be an effective way of "keeping in touch" with the unit's work and finding out about its problems, in which case it falls under the role of communicating. Or it may be done to demonstrate involvement and commitment with others in the unit, in which case it falls under the role of culture-building in the role of leading.

Dealing takes place in terms of deals and negotiations outside the unit. Again, these are two sides of the same coin, in that managers negotiate in order to "do deals" and also negotiate once the deal is done. And again there is no shortage of evidence on the importance of dealing in managerial work. In large organizations, senior managers may have all kinds of specialized negotiators supporting them – lawyers for contracts and labour relations specialists for union bargaining – yet that does not release them from having to spend considerable time on negotiations themselves, especially when critical moments arise. After all, they are the ones who have the authority to commit the resources of their unit, and it is they who are the nerve centres of its information as well as the energy centres of its activity, not to mention the conceptual centres of its strategy. All around the circles, therefore, action connects to people who connect to information, which connects to the frame.

THE WELL-ROUNDED JOB OF MANAGING

The best-known writers of management all seem to emphasize one aspect of the job, in the terms we have now: "doing" for Tom Peters, "conceiving" for Michael Porter, "leading" for Warren Bennis, "controlling" for Henri Fayol, and so on.[10] Now it can be appreciated why all may be somewhat wrong: heeding the advice of any one of them must lead to the lopsided practice of managerial work. Like an unbalanced wheel at resonant frequency, the job may risk flying out of control. That is why it is important to show all of the components of managerial work on a single integrated diagram, as in Figure 1.6, to remind people, at a glance, that these components form one job and cannot be separated.

Acceptance of Tom Peters' urgings, "Don't think, do,' could lead to the centrifugal explosion of the job, as it flies off in all directions, free of a strong frame anchoring it at the core. But acceptance of the spirit of Michael Porter's opposite urgings that what matters most is conception of the frame, especially of strategic positions, could produce a result that is no better: centripetal implosion, as the job closes in on itself cerebrally, disconnected from outer actions. Thinking is heavy and can wear down the incumbent, while acting is light and cannot keep him or her in place.

Only together do they provide the balance that seems so characteristic of effective management.

Too much leading produces a job free of content – aimless, frameless and actionless – while too much linking produces a job detached from its internal roots, public relations instead of public service. The manager who only communicates or only conceives never gets anything done, while the manager who only "does" ends up doing it all alone. And, of course, we all know what happens to managers who believe their job is merely to control.

A couple of bad puns may thus make for good practice. The manager must practice a well-rounded job. Or, if you prefer, anyone who wants to hold this job must swallow the whole pill, which may not be a bad metaphor, since the outer coating of doing provides the immediate effect, while each successive layer in this time-release capsule provides deeper, less accessible, but more long-term effects. The different roles are somewhat substitutable, to be sure. A manager can, for example, push employees through controlling by systems or else pull them through leading by culture. But, more important, these roles are complementary.

In fact, while we may be able to separate the components of this job conceptually, they cannot be separated behaviourally. In other words, it may be useful, even necessary, to delineate the parts of the job for purposes of design, selection, training and support. But this job cannot be practised as a set of independent parts. As suggested, the core is a kind of magnet that holds the rest together, while the communication ring acts as a membrane that allows the flow of information between inner thinking and outer behaviour, which tie people to action.

Indeed, the most interesting aspects of this job may well fall on the edges, between the component parts. For example, Andrew Grove, as CEO of Intel, has described what he did as "nudging," a perfect blend of controlling, leading and doing.[11] This can mean pushing people, tangibly but not aggressively, and in effect doing or controlling, together with leading. There are similar edges between the inside and the outside, between thinking and behaving, and between communicating and controlling, as we shall see.

Managers who try to "deal" without "doing" inevitably get themselves into trouble. Just consider all those chief executives who "did the deal," acquired the company or whatever, and then dropped it into the laps of others for execution. Likewise, it makes no more sense to conceive and then fail to lead and do – as has been the tendency in so-called "strategic planning," where controlling has often been considered sufficient for "implementation" – than it makes sense to do or to lead without thinking through the frame in which to embed these activities.

MANAGING IN STYLE

To describe the various components that make up the job of managing as integrated, infused and well rounded is not to imply that all managers do all of them with equal emphasis. Managerial work does vary, according to the needs of a particular job and the approach of its particular incumbent. Different managers end up emphasizing different things in different ways. The key for every manager is to find the appropriate balance among the roles for a particular period of time.

Most obviously, managers in different contexts have to emphasize different roles. For example, the managers of autonomous professionals, as in hospitals or universities, tend to favour linking over leading (let alone controlling), since professionals tend to come to their work naturally empowered. In other words, these people need little encouragement or supervision, although they do require considerable external support. However, when experts must work in teams, as in some research laboratories or in professional sports, leadership becomes rather critical, particularly at the group level. Entrepreneurs, in contrast, who run their own businesses, tend to emphasize doing and dealing alongside conceiving, as they involve themselves deeply in specific issues. Interestingly, the same thing tends to be true of first-line managers, even in conventional big businesses – for example, foremen in factories who must resolve steady streams of operating problems. Senior executives of large diversified firms, on the other hand, likely give greater attention to controlling, particularly to their systems of performance control and their decisions to authorize major capital expenditures.

Of course, regardless of the context, individual managers are often personally predisposed to favour particular roles or aspects of the job. Considering this from the inside out, we can, for example, distinguish a *conceptual* style of management, which focuses on the development of the frame; an *administrative* style, which concerns itself primarily with controlling; an *interpersonal* style, which favours leading on the inside or linking on the outside; and an *action* style, which is concerned mainly with tangible doing and dealing. And, as we move out in this order, the overall style of managing can be described as less opaque, more visible.

Even in how they respond to requests, managers can exhibit subtle yet significant variations in style. Asked for advice by an employee, a manager may respond as a communicator ("Payroll has some data on this."), a controller ("Don't do it."), or a leader ("How do you feel about it?"). Of course, the doer may say "Just leave it with me." All kinds of opportunities arise in managing to substitute, combine and give nuance to the different roles.

Regardless of which roles or aspects of the job a particular manager emphasizes, his or her personal style is manifested particularly in how these are performed. We have already seen this, for example, in different approaches to linking at the extremes – the sieve, the lead, the sponge – and the different approaches to conceiving the frame. Similarly, we saw different predispositions to leading, favouring the individual, group or unit level. Other obvious variations in style can be delineated according to how each of the remaining components of the model might be carried out.

A final aspect of managerial style has to do with the interrelationships among the various components of managerial work. For example, an important distinction can be made between deductive and inductive approaches to managerial work. The former proceeds from the core out, as the conceived frame is implemented through scheduling that uses information to drive people to get action done. We can call this a cerebral style of managing, highly deliberate, noting that it has been popular, from the early POSDCORB writers to the current proponents of strategic planning and bottom-line thinking. But there is an alternate, emergent view of the management process as well, which proceeds inductively, from the outer surface to the inner core. We might label it an insightful style. As Karl Weick puts it, managers act in order to think. They try things to gain experience, retain what works and, then, by interpreting the results, gradually evolve their frames.[12]

Of course, the preferred approach may well vary with context as well as with personal inclination. When a situation is well understood, the cerebral side seems to make sense, while, under conditions of ambiguity, the insightful style may be more appropriate. Part of our problem in recent years, in educating managers as well as in their own practice, has been a predisposition towards the cerebral style in situations of increasing ambiguity that require inductive insight. Even "doing" is one step removed from the action: how then is a manager who relies on controlling, three steps removed, to come to serious grips with real problems in an organization?

Clearly, there is an enormous variety of possible contexts within which management can be practised. But just as clearly, perhaps, a model such as the one presented here can help to order them and so come to grips with the difficult requirements of designing managerial jobs, selecting the right people to fill them, and training them accordingly. It is in this spirit that we turn now to eight days in the lives of managers in the Government of Canada.

2

Managing on the Edges[13]

Many of the most interesting things, say the biologists, happen on the Edges – on the interface between the woods and the field, the land and the sea. There, living organisms encounter dynamic conditions that give rise to untold variety. Scientific studies of bird populations reveal that forest-edge species are generally more abundant than those which confine their territory to the interior of the forest. The inter-tidal zone, meanwhile, that thin ribbon which separates the land from the sea, supports a plurality of life uniquely adapted to both air and water.

Variety, perhaps, but there is tension as well. The flora of the meadows, as they approach the woodlands, find themselves coping with increasingly unfavorable conditions: the sunlight they need might be lacking, and the soil no longer feels right. ... The Edges, in short, might abound with life, but each living form must fight for its own.[14]

When I spoke to Gord Irwin late in the day, I asked him about a most curious division of labour – the separation between the "front country" that he manages in the Banff National Park and the "back country" that a colleague of his looks after – he laughed. They tried to pin that down in Ottawa, he said, designating the dividing line as fifty metres off the road. In fact, the back-country people look after the trails right from the road, while his responsibility for emergency response includes the entire park! Gord presumably had this responsibility for historical reasons – he spent a great part of his career developing the park's renowned expertise in mountain rescue. But one could also argue that the helicopters are kept and serviced in, and leave from, the front-country.

This story serves not only as a wonderful illustration of what I observed throughout these three days – best described as managing on the edges – but as an apt metaphor as well. For here, ironically, despite the ambiguities in pinning down this physical edge, it is rather crystal clear compared with some of the other, more symbolic edges – administrative and political – encountered in my observation of managers in the parks. Going out to a mountain park thinking of nature and forgetting about human nature sets one up for quite a surprise!

I had already observed a number of other managers in government, in delicate political contexts, such as the RCMP and the Justice Department. Yet none of this prepared me for the intensity of the political situation faced by the managers of the parks. Far from Ottawa, in or near these superb natural settings, politics seem to come out much more sharply and overtly. Perhaps the edges are clearer out here.

Gord at one point mentioned a "bear jam." "What's that?" I asked. "A traffic jam caused by a bear. A bear sometimes ambles down the road, the tourists stop, some even get out of the cars to get better pictures!" Then the truckers and other motorists, who depend on the same road to cross the continental divide, stew. This is only the most physically evident form of confrontation between factions who compete for different uses of the park.

The most politically evident form of confrontation, during these days of observation and for many years before, had been between the developers and the environmentalists. Both, of course, have their agendas – one to use the parks for their commercial purposes or, perhaps as they might put it, to make it more easily accessible to tourists, or to consumers of wood products, or workers in need of employment, etc. – the other to preserve the natural state of the parks. These can be competing agendas, of course, but what has turned natural friction into almost overt war in recent years is the propensity of both sides to view this as a "zero-sum game" (if you win, I lose). So some of the environmentalists, at least, are continually taking last stands against the developers, looking for any pretense to stop any further development, while some of the corresponding developers get their glee out of slipping something past the environmentalists.

Sitting between all this are the managers of the parks, watched closely by the press looking for good stories, the politicians wishing to accommodate their supporters while minimizing the political fallout, and the public servants in the capital seeking to avoid scandal. Watching it all unfold in the field can get one thinking about whether the real "civilization" is not in the back-country!

The burning issue at this time was a proposed new parking lot for a ski hill in Banff National Park. Its owner was a rather aggressive businessman who was well connected to the then ruling Progressive Conservative Party, as well as the then sitting member of Parliament from this area, herself also with a reputation for being rather aggressive. The parking lot was being hotly contested by environmental groups that claimed it would block a major traverse used by several kinds of animals and add to the accumulating loss of old-growth forest. The issue began in the front-country. Gord's unit worked on an initial report and made recommendations. But it quickly escalated, not just past the front-country and the park itself, but beyond the Western Region and into the whole Parks Service. From there, it went into the national headquarters of the Department of the Environment, to which Parks Canada then reported, and from there to the political level. Finally, the whole "file" was managed in Ottawa. All this over a tiny plot of land in a country of ten million square kilometres.

Not that these three managers, whom I observed over these three days in succession, were freed from the issue. Quite the contrary, the issue was a central concern in the Park and regional headquarters, on those days as well. So one begins to get an idea of just how delicate managing on the edges can be, between the developers and environmentalists, the politicians and the public servants, the department and the Parks Service, the Parks Service headquarters in Ottawa and its regions, and this particular region and its parks, leaving aside the truckers and the tourists in the front-country, or the tourists from the front-country and the bears from the back, let alone the edges with ourselves.[15]

Eighteen parks, with nine million visitors annually, a staff of 2,200 people, and a budget of $110,000,000 fell under the authority of Sandy Davis, regional director general of the Western Region of Parks Canada. She holds an MBA and had worked in the Correctional Service in Ottawa before joining the Parks Service in 1988, but now worked in a modern government office building in Calgary. Sandy was considered to be someone who got things done and as being sympathetic to the legacy of the parks. Charlie Zinkan was superintendent of one of these parks, Banff, perhaps the best known internationally and, in fact, the origin of the whole Canadian parks system.[16] Charlie worked in a stunning stone building, a landmark that looked down on to the main street of the town of Banff and then out to the mountains beyond. He still wore his warden outfit to work, having spent his career in the parks he knew intimately. Gord Irwin was a park warden in Banff National Park, in charge of the "front-country." He worked in a prefabricated-type building on the outskirts of the town of Banff, part of a small complex that houses some of Parks' equipment, such as trucks and snow-removal machines.

Gord reported to Charlie who reported to Sandy. So, while some of the differences in their work may have reflected the differences in their physical settings, the fact that the three shared this need to manage on some similar edges but at different levels in a formal hierarchy makes it interesting to discuss their work together. Hence I shall proceed by describing their days, first chronologically and then conceptually, before turning to an overall conceptual interpretation and comparison of their common situation.

SANDY DAVIS, REGIONAL DIRECTOR, WESTERN REGION, PARKS CANADA, CALGARY, 12 AUGUST 1993

I arrived at Sandy Davis' Calgary office at 8:30 a.m. for what she called a fairly normal "in the office" day. We chatted for about twenty minutes while she described the running of the parks: these are municipalities of sorts, a good deal of the work involving the daily routine of removing the garbage, ploughing the roads, and ticketing speeding motorists.

Her daily briefing followed at 8:50 a.m., with her own reports and with a discussion ranging from information-sharing to scheduling to making certain decisions. It proceeded briskly, with Sandy taking a rather hands-on posture of advising and sometimes directing. She briefed the others on her recent contacts with Ottawa, and then discussed some brewing problems of staff appointments and a protest in one park that could turn violent. "Any other 'hot' issues?" Sandy asked at one point, to which she received the reply, "There's a couple of lukewarm ones." These consisted of a letter that went to a minister about the rents paid by the wardens for their housing in the parks, a railways spill, and a trail closure in a park (the goats come down this time of year, followed by the bears who might menace the people), about which the owners of a nearby lodge had written hoping the closure would not be permanent. The group also discussed links with Heritage Canada people in Vancouver, since Parks Canada had recently been shifted from the Environment Department to the newly created one of Heritage Canada. The meeting ended at 9:50 a.m.

After some brief encounters in the hall, a more formal meeting was convened with Sandy and the region's two planning people, as well as the director of National Parks Operations, who arrived later. There were four items on the written agenda. The first concerned the construction of a new facility, and again Sandy factored in the political dimension, expressing concern about the level of the expenditure just before an election. The next item seemed even more delicate: the need to approve the draft of a newsletter announcing a government–native band agreement on a new wilderness site. Sandy was concerned that it be checked carefully. She also suggested they try to get the minister to make the public announcement.

Item 3 – "my favourite topic," said Sandy – concerned the "Four Mountain Parks Planning Program," another newsletter announcing a five-year review of the plans that guide the major parks and inviting public participation. Sandy was clearly trying to pre-empt problems here, insisting that she be kept very closely briefed and suggesting some specific changes including mention of the "heritage" aspect, which, given the new ministry of the parks, she thought was "absolutely critical." Sandy also expressed her feelings and said, "I'm strictly from a political standpoint here, [we need] to meet with ... and show [the draft newsletter] to the [Progressive Conservative] caucus before [the letter] goes out."

Item 4 concerned the "Strategic Plan: Program Update." A twenty-page draft called "Defining Our Destiny – Leadership through Excellence" was handed out. It included sections on the mandate, the mission, a vision statement and ten "values" that ranged from pride in heritage to respect for "strategic thinking linked to strategic action" and eight "strategic priorities and objectives" described at some length, including "effectively managing protected areas," "commemorating and protecting cultural heritage" and "organizational excellence."

The meeting ended at 11:03 a.m., at which point Sandy turned to me and said, "Henry, let's go for a walk!" The building was being renovated in an open, cheerful way, and, as we walked, Sandy greeted many people and introduced herself (and me) to the ones she didn't know. We were back in the office in about fifteen minutes, and then a call came through that she had placed earlier to the new assistant deputy minister, her boss. She welcomed him to his job, suggested a trip to Ottawa to brief him on the issues and commented on a number of them, including the parking lot. She mentioned the plan for the four western parks as well as the meeting with the caucus later in the month, and she told him about a possible court challenge.

This was followed by a conference call among her people, including Charlie Zinkan at Banff, about the parking lot. They discussed location and a report being prepared. At one point, Sandy turned to me and said, "If you want to know what the biggest waste of a manager's time is, it's this sort of thing," referring to the level of detail of the conversation. Sandy intervened at one point to reiterate how contentious the issue was, how the minister might react to it, and what was her own preferred course of action. "As soon as a final recommendation is made, both sides are prepared to go to war." At 12:30 p.m., we were off to lunch, accompanied by the group that had attended the early morning meeting. "A lot of my job is mediating," Sandy said over lunch, and when I drew the model of managerial work, she pointed to the centre and said, "I'm that point in the hourglass."

Back at 2:25 p.m. – including ten-minute drives each way and discussions over lunch – Sandy turned briefly to her mail, signing bills and letters, etc. "The only things I sign are the things only I can sign," she said.

"The amount of mail I see is quite small," and she estimated that she spent about forty per cent of her time dealing with issues, half of it outside the unit, and considerable time with her own staff, including about thirty per cent visiting the parks. A few minutes later, Sandy went into an "open forum," which she chaired, of whomever wished to come from the regional office. Nine people showed up, mostly new, younger members of the staff, a few of whom Sandy had not yet met. She introduced herself to them and announced, "This is your session. Ask anything you like. No repercussions," and then turned to their questions as well as commenting on the specifics and the values of the operation. "How do you new guys like working for Parks Canada?" she asked at one point. "Great," "like the atmosphere," and, from one person who wanted to work in a park itself, "The closer you get to the parks, the more relaxed people are." Someone asked Sandy about her job: "I'm not sure what you do. Heard there is supposed to be a clash of thunder behind it [referring to her energetic nature]. So what do you do and how much power do you have?" Sandy talked about being a civil servant concerned with the delivery of program operations and about her responsibility for budgets, staffing and development. She ducked the second question by saying "it depends how you want to define power!" She was not at all rushed, and, after an hour, as the questions petered out, she thanked everyone, expressed her availability to them, and said good-bye to each by name.

At 3:45 p.m., we went into a meeting of all the region's directors, ten people in all, called, it turned out, to give them an opportunity to meet me (the Mintzberg Principle at work!). I raised the issue of managing in the middle, between Parks' operations and the Ottawa headquarters, and a number of people pointed out that they began at the base of Parks operations and have subsequently moved back and forth between there and the regional headquarters. Sandy was the only one to have moved from Ottawa to the regional headquarters. I also asked a question about "empowering" versus controlling, and Sandy talked about "a foundation [in the strategic plans, etc.] that creates a common understanding." That reduces the need for direct controlling, she said, although frustration was also expressed with the "paper trail" required in government operations. When I expressed my surprise at coming out to study the fresh air of the parks and finding the extent of the political conflict, commenting that this was perhaps reflective only of that particular morning, one of the senior directors said "That's pretty well it!" The discussion lasted for about twenty-five minutes, and then Sandy briefed everyone on a few other issues for another few minutes.

Back in her office at 4:30 p.m., Sandy tried to call back the member of Parliament for Banff, who had left a message. Then three of her staff people came in to review budgets. With a mention of a park that was running over budget, Sandy said "You call him and tell him that if he wants to be working for the Parks Department next year, he had better do something. This is a first warning; if I call, he'll be in my office." Meanwhile a call came in from a senior official in the Heritage Department in Ottawa, whom Sandy briefed for about five minutes on a meeting that was held, including the "animosity" that was expressed during it. They then turned back to the budget review, with Sandy also commenting on the call, and at 5:00 p.m., they left and the regular day ended, although we stayed and talked for some time.

When I mentioned her sensitivity to the political dimension and how she seemed to overlay that dimension on the administrative process, Sandy said "That's my value-added." But could not the broad view become the disconnected view, I asked. "I work very hard at that. I know the parks and I know the issues. I've been to every one of the parks numerous times." The difficulty, of course, is the "dichotomous mandate of protection and preservation," which she and her people try to make into one continuum through the concept of "sustainability." But as this day and the next two made clear, that is no easy task.

Managing Up

On this day, Sandy appeared to be a linker above all, overlaying the political dimension on the issues and operations of her region. She was certainly sensitive and astute about these issues and highly informed with regard to them. In this sense, what she did could be described as "managing up" in terms of conventional notions of hierarchy, to the senior levels of her service and department in Ottawa, and then on to the political level. Her focus could thus be described as a kind of horizontal edge hovering over her region.

Networking and communicating, especially outside her unit, notably keeping Ottawa informed, seemed to be the critical functions for her, used to strengthen and protect her unit but also to help it deal with the highly contentious issues that bombard it. The parks are places where certain opposing forces square off, and the people who run the parks necessarily become the mediators, as Sandy pointed out.

But this did not seem to translate into a large amount of dealing as such. Clearly there has to be some of this in the negotiations with forceful outside interests, although I saw only indirect evidence of it this day, but perhaps not all that much doing of self-initiated deals, per se. Linking would seem to be more of a reactive activity here, although the way Sandy did it could hardly be described as passive. In fact, when I asked her if she saw herself as a "referee" in these disputes, she preferred the label "objective intervener" instead, an advocate for scientifically based sustainable development, which she saw as a reconciliation of the competing interests.

With regard to managing into her unit, according to what I saw and had indicated to me, Sandy seemed to be less a doer than an indirect controller and leader. The controlling role was clearly evident in the budget discussions, both at a general systems level and a specific level and in the clear directives she issued on numerous occasions throughout the day. She knew what she wanted, and how she wanted it done, and she was certainly not shy about expressing these intentions. Yet, she herself seemed to place more emphasis on the systems aspect of the controlling role. For example, she claimed that a tool such as the systems plan gives people a basis for consistency and so reduced her need to control more directly. But as I saw it, there was still the considerable issuing of specific directives.

Leading came through most clearly, and in rather pure form, in that meeting with the new staff, an impressive exercise in how to bring people on board, as well as in her encouraging comments to a number of the regional people during the day.

Still, at times Sandy came close to inside doing too. For example, when expressing herself on a new problem brewing in one of the parks, the line between issuing directives of how she wanted something done and actually taking charge of the doing of it seemed to become rather thin. And as the main person who factored the political dimension into the handling of issues – thereby connecting governmental politics to administrative process – she came rather close to internal doing as well. But controlling and leading more than doing still seem to describe her inside style of managing. In other words, her style of management was more evident at the information and people levels than at the action level per se.

Figure 2.1 shows a matrix of styles associated with the frame of a manager's job (discussed in Chapter 1): the frame may be selected by the manager or imposed on him or her, and it can be vaguely or sharply defined. A frame that is clearly defined and externally imposed, for example by the minister's office or the Treasury Board, gives rise to a *driven* style of management; one that is clearly defined but self-selected by the manager is called *determined*. A vague frame that is imposed leads to a *passive* style, and one that is self-selected is called *opportunistic*.

Sandy is evidently a highly determined woman and rather driven in her work. She has a sharp frame in her mind with regard to her purpose in general and to specific issues in particular, each of those issues themselves being rather sharply delineated. This frame was imposed partly by

Figure 2.1 *Matrix of Styles*

		Vague	Sharp
Frame	Imposed	Passive	Driven
	Selected	Opportunist	Determined

the nature of the job itself and partly selected by Sandy to reflect her own view of the job.

In overall style, Sandy Davis would seem to be rather close to the true "professional manager." Her determination suggests more of a deliberate, deductive approach to the conceiving of strategy than an emergent, inductive approach, likewise a rather cerebral orientation.

The clearest evidence of this appeared in the "strategic planning" activities of the day, obviously championed by her, with its mandate, mission, vision, etc. There is an irony in this, however. In this fast-moving political context in which people are forced to be dependent on soft data, quick impressions, rapid moves and good contacts, all of this seems antithetical to these formal systems and statements. Sandy Davis would likely argue that these are complementary, yet it is far from obvious how one reconciles "Our mission: To sustain the integrity, health, diversity, majesty and beauty of Western Canada's Cultural and National Heritage"[17] with a knock-down, drag-out battle over a parking lot.

CHARLIE ZINKAN, SUPERINTENDENT, BANFF NATIONAL PARK, 13 AUGUST 1993

The headquarters of Banff National Park sits just beyond and above the heart of the town of Banff, in the impressive building originally built as a spa and recently restored. Charlie Zinkan occupies a large office that looks down Banff Avenue. But belying that image is a low-key atmosphere, easy, friendly and very much giving the impression that one was now in the parks. Charlie wore a Parks uniform, but some of the other people there wore jeans.

Charlie suggested I come in at 8:00 a.m., when his daily one-hour French class began. Since French was required for his bilingual position, he thought the class could be considered part of his managerial work!

The class ended at 9:05 a.m., and we continued to chat (in English). He expected a light load this day, although "some days it is almost impossible to escape this place." There used to be seven layers of management in the park, he said, but now, with a budget of $10,000,000, including 270 people full-time, and another 500 in the summer, plus about 30 to 50 managers, it was down to three levels, sometimes four. There were a series of units dealing with central administration (finance, human resources, planning, communication) and others with park services (leases, roads, campgrounds, law enforcement and public safety, conservation, and the front- and back-country services).

At 9:20 a.m., in the midst of going over the chart, the man in charge of program services came in for about five minutes. He talked of a conflict with a developer, referred to "licking our wounds" and said that he "just wanted to let [Charlie] know" what had been done, the details of which Charlie was in agreement. "Better we did it than you," he said. They also discussed a problem with the accounting system.

Then a call came from a manager of a power company. He was concerned with environmentalists' efforts to stop an energy-supply project and their request for a meeting. Charlie explained some of the concerns of the environmental groups and suggested to the caller that early September might be best for the meeting. The manager continued, referring to the role of his company as one of non-involvement in the management of the park and as one that provided services in the park. He also referred to a colleague's tendency towards saber rattling, trying to come in at the top, and intervening politically at the federal level. The call lasted twenty-one minutes, during most of which time Charlie listened politely while his caller said what he wanted to say.

In between other calls, about scheduling mostly, Charlie and I chatted. Before the reorganization, morale was a serious problem in the park, Charlie said. It was a struggle to get the managers to be less directive, especially given the political pressures to centralize decision-making and the fact that science is not really up to the ecological questions that get raised. Charlie felt that classic top–down control of government was just incompatible with the highly educated people attracted to work in the parks, even with those people doing simple jobs in the hope of moving on to more interesting ones. You "have to be careful when talking 'empowerment' to these people," he said. "We have mechanics reading the Harvard Business Review!" The people in the field are committed to their own values: "These are the lone rangers in the organization."

He described Banff Park as especially sensitive, given its history and visibility. Here, particularly, is where everything comes together: tourists, developers, a transcontinental highway, etc. Charlie described three parks, two in the U.S. – Yellowstone and Yosemite – and Banff as "lightning rods" for these concerns, the ones that have influenced world development policies: "There will be weeks and weeks when issues drive my life." The ecological interests of the Bow Valley of Banff Park may be impossible to manage, he suggested. He referred specifically to the conflicts between the Alberta members of Parliament, all from the Progressive Conservative Party at the time, and the ENGOs (environmental nongovernment organizations), especially concerning the parking lot but also about the proposals to "twin" the Trans-Canada Highway so that it could carry more traffic and so avoid those "bear jams."

At 10:30 a.m., Charlie began to sign leasehold documents, a required formality, and Sandy Davis called at 10:40 a.m. about a conversation she had with the local member of Parliament, asking Charlie to speak to that person, too, which he did immediately. "I'm just following up," he said, telling the woman about a consulting firm that had been hired by Ottawa and about a meeting with the ski hill owner and their "very positive working relationship." They also discussed arrangements between the town of Banff and the federal government, on whose land the entire town sits. That call ended just before 11:00 a.m., but it was followed by another, also of about fifteen minutes, from the head of operations at the ski centre. He expressed concerns about the environmental report and explained his boss's position. He discussed different possible alignments for the road and asked about Charlie's concerns.

Charlie then met with the head of a bungalow camping ground to discuss Indian land claims near the facility. The tone of this encounter was quite different, with the visitor mostly listening quietly as Charlie explained the claim and the government's position very carefully, trying to alleviate the man's anxieties. Twenty-six years earlier, a lawyer had told him about the claim and that he could eventually be ousted, but no one had ever come back to discuss it, nor had he sought information about it. He was grateful to Charlie for taking the initiative to explain it and clearly expressed relief. He raised one final issue, about another edge. The railroad crosses the continental divide in this area, and their engineers tend to blow their whistles as they do, even during the night. "We're supposed to be providing a wilderness experience and here we have this noise pollution!" Could Charlie do anything about this? Charlie talked about having to discuss this with the railroad people: "Maybe I'll find out who the vice-president for public relations is and offer a gift certificate of a free night to listen to the whistles," he joked.

After a brief lunch, Charlie and I headed off to the park's ranch at the far end of town so that Charlie could arrange to do some riding to get into shape for a five-day trip he was going on into the back-country. That part of the park is regularly patrolled on horseback. Charlie wanted to have a look at that part of the park and be "visible" there. But this was not just "management by riding around"; he was taking along several wardens, two RCMP people, and a businessman, as an opportunity to exchange ideas. Back at the office, just after 3:00 p.m., after stopping briefly at the operations headquarters, where I would spend the next day, the regional specialist in public safety came in to talk about cost-recovery for emergency services (search and rescue). He had spoken with other groups (such as the Coast Guard) about this, and had some ideas. One was to impose a surcharge on all the vehicles entering the park, a kind of compulsory insurance, although it would be preferable, if much more difficult, to charge the actual recipient of the service. He wanted Charlie's approval to "pitch" the idea to others.

After another brief meeting on space for equipment storage, we took a break in the meetings to look at Charlie's schedule in a broader sense, first his agenda of scheduled meetings for the rest of that week (this was Friday). Every day began with French class. On Monday there had been a briefing on training and a team-building session, plus discussion of a problem a manager was having with some of his people. A Japanese attaché at the Washington embassy had come in to discuss some issues, such as Japanese commercial ownership in Banff village, which Charlie saw as a kind of VIP visit. It might be noted that Lake Louise, within Banff Park, is a site revered by the Japanese. Charlie had also met with the owner of the ski hill and with his own managers on real-property management. On Tuesday there had been a conference call on the future of "hot pools," a "zero-based budgeting" review exercise, more attention to the parking lot, a telephone interview on a survey with the Office of the Auditor General in Ottawa, a meeting with a local organization about a space exchange and, in the evening, a Heritage Department meeting. Wednesday had included WordPerfect training and lunch with Sandy in Calgary, which is about an hour and a half drive away, concerning the parking lot issue, followed by another evening concerning the Heritage Department. Thursday had included that conference call on the parking lot ("You can see how one issue can dominate chunks of my time") and meetings in Lake Louise, almost a one-hour drive the other way, on union issues, and with a hotel owner concerned about pedestrians crossing his property.

The following week's scheduled meetings included an "agenda-driven" executive meeting on planning, a meeting with the ski hill owner and a consultant hired to look at different possible alignments of the parking lot, a visit by Sandy, a reception at the Banff Cultural Centre, a follow-up call from the auditor general's office, lunch with a U.S. congressman on national parks conservation, and a parade at a cadet camp, where Charlie had a ceremonial role to play.

We then chatted about his job and his need to play a reactive role with regard to some of the projects initiated by the developers as well as others initiated by the park's people themselves. With delayering, Charlie found that his job had become heavier, with many more people reporting to him. As he put it in comments to me later, "Perhaps the problem is empowerment down to some managers who lack skills and confidence and consequently try to delegate upwards."

At 4:45 p.m., a consultant to the region came in. He and Charlie chatted about management in the service, until 5:25 p.m., when Charlie's day ended.

Managing Out

At one point, Charlie said that he saw himself in the same hourglass as Sandy, with the outside pressures flowing down from above and passing on to the park's operations below. But while this edge was no less evident in Charlie's day – in fact more pointedly so – there seemed to be a rather different edge at play here. Sandy was more focused on factoring in the political dimension from above, namely from Parks' headquarters, the ministry and the rest of the government in Ottawa. Charlie, in contrast, was much more involved with the specific conflicts in the park, on either side, if you like: between a campground and an Indian band, as well as a noisy railroad; between the truckers, who wanted the road twinned, and the ENGOs, which did not; between the injured climbers who receive the rescue services and all the park's visitors, who might be asked to pay for it; and, of course, between that famous parking lot sitting between the ski hill operator and the ENGOs. These conflicts may have been political, and some could easily have escalated to the formal level of governmental politics, but a number, such as that between the campground and the railroad, hit tangibly and directly on Charlie as the manager of the park.

Thus, linking loomed large indeed in Charlie's job that day. He was not dealing, in the sense of negotiating final settlements, although there were hints of all kinds of these in progress. Rather, he was representing his unit to the outside world, transmitting to others in the unit the information and influence that he received. Charlie took a proactive stance, at least with regard to informing, when he met with the campground operator, and took more of a reactive stance when he listened to some of the other issues.

As Charlie implied, the amount of linking required probably preempted some attention to the other roles. Thus, I saw a bit of controlling here, but little internal leading per se, although some leading came out in the agenda of the other days, and most of the communicating he did was tied to the external linking activities, namely acting as the park's spokesperson.

The frame of Charlie's job seems clear enough. He pointed to the strategic plan as a guiding force, within which he sought to handle the external pressures. But frame and plan are not necessarily easily reconcilable. At one point, Charlie said that the problems of managing some of the ecological concerns made the technical execution of the official mandate difficult and, thus, subject to external challenge.

If a single word is required to describe Charlie's management style that day, mediating might well be the best word. He sat between all these interests, necessarily responding to many, as delicately as possible, although taking a proactive stance on some as well. Charlie certainly appeared more low-key than Sandy, less inclined to impose a strong stamp on what he passed through the system, or maybe he did so less overtly. But that might well have been in the nature of his job too, even within his unit. He complained when signing leasehold documents that the system should allow for more delegation. This came up just after our discussion about the nature of management in government, especially with regard to the high levels of education in the parks and the "lone ranger" quality of the operating staff. In a sense, the park superintendent takes the heat for his people, much as I found in a hospital where the medical chiefs do so for the doctors so that they can concentrate on their specialized work.[18] Thus Charlie's sideways edge converts into a horizontal edge too, between management and the operations.

GORD IRWIN, PARK WARDEN (FRONT-COUNTRY), BANFF NATIONAL PARK, 14 AUGUST 1993

Gord Irwin came in on Saturday, not to accommodate me but because weekends are key working times in the summer. Corresponding to that arbitrary line that the Ottawa people wanted to impose between front- and back-country, Gord said he found working 9:00 a.m to 5:00 p.m. strange in a way, claiming he needed to access people at odd hours.

The focus of this job was clearly different from the outset (8:30 a.m.). Gord was just back from a mountain rescue course and spent the first half-hour putting ice axes, cords and crampons, etc. into their respective boxes. Finally the mountains! Well, almost.

During this, he talked proudly of the worldwide reputation of this search-and-rescue team and discussed the leadership aspect of the course, especially how, in this context, leadership is not a fixed position but a function of who has particular skills at particular times. The search-and-rescue team is viewed as an élite group, he said, but, in life and death situations, the level of expertise and knowledge, as well as trust, responsibility and camaraderie, is that much more important. Ultimately, leadership here is a team-building exercise, he felt.

Walking back to the office, Gord chatted with a couple of his people, briefing the wildlife specialist on the dart, the dose and the procedure he and others used to tranquilize elk (in order to get them out of town and into the back-country). They also discussed the trapping of grizzly bears, and his experience in the training school. "It's that public expression we have to think about," Gord said with regard to the animals, raising, this time in a general sense, the edge between his work and the public.

Between Gord's comings and goings out of his office, to chat informally with people, we discussed his job. It had been reorganized since February, although he had only come into it in June. Before that, Lake Louise had a parallel structure, its own front- and back-country managers, etc. The new structure used "product lines" instead of geographical areas, so that now he had to look after the Lake Louise area as well as Banff, although each still had a supervisor for the four busy months of the year. That meant he had twenty-three people reporting to him, which he thought difficult, given that a lot of the work involved the settlement of disputes and the assignment of tasks.

Much of this, Gord said, was based on budgets, which are "moving targets" that make realistic planning difficult. The intention was to flatten the organization, but here, where this had a very tangible impact, he felt it did not work well in practice: people need someone to turn to for help, such as for a second opinion, a kind of accessible mentor. Power over decision-making is, in effect, decentralized managerially but then usurped politically, which makes things difficult for the operating staff. Gord mentioned the parking lot at this point. He noted another set of edges in this regard too, in and near the town, that upset the local residents – the problems that arise for them when the bull elk rut in the fall and become aggressive and when the cow elk calve in the spring, sometimes doing so near town where they are relatively safe from predators, who are less comfortable around people (an edge for the elk!).

At 10:15 a.m., Gord turned to his e-mail, commenting that once you become a manager, your names goes on mailing lists and it becomes "difficult to get meaningful work done." "Someone in Ottawa can hit a button and get on the e-mail of every staff person in Canada!" Once he came back after six days to 176 new messages! This time, five days away, he had forty new messages. They comprised some direct material, including a question about how to divide people for an upcoming teamwork training seminar, a request for information concerning a film-making project, and several messages about scheduling.

Then, eventually, Gord began scanning the messages quickly, until "this one is a bit of a time bomb" – about a problem in the campgrounds between animal habitation and human drinking. Others dealt with patrol-staff availability, a housing-allocation problem for staff in Lake Louise, "a meeting I dread, a free for-all," and training in hoof care and the shoeing of horses. It was now 11:26 a.m., and the forty messages had been reduced to ten.

A call then came in from the supervisor at Lake Louise. They chatted for a couple of minutes about various things, including the search-and-rescue school. Then Gord turned to his computer for a few minutes, until a staffer, full-time on mountain rescue, came in, and they reviewed some technical rescue systems in comparison with what appeared in the manuals. The staffer left at 12:15 p.m., and then Gord and I talked about management issues.

Gord felt that mission statements, if substantial and not just buzzwords for Ottawa, can be a helpful guide in dealing with the difficult trade-offs, while policies are not – they tend to be too tight and can go out-of-date quickly. Ironically, a few minutes earlier, while Gord was on the telephone, I overheard a conversation in the hall about "gearing up for a new mission and a new vision and all this and that. All they do is just crank this [stuff] out. It makes it look like they're doing something. We have our little mission: it sure keeps a few people busy! ... Anyway, I'll leave you to your e-mail." We discussed the hierarchy of the parks and some of the currently popular buzzwords at its higher levels "win-win," "empowerment," "flattening the organization", "stewardship" and, of course, "heritage." Two days earlier, at regional headquarters, I heard someone say: "Did you go back through [the planning document headed for Ottawa] and write down the word 'heritage' everywhere you could ?" Over lunch, we also discussed leadership, with Gord describing a form of his job quite different from that of the formal hierarchy, revolving around work teams and being informal as much as formal.

At 1:30 p.m., Gord placed a call to a consultant about setting up the groups for a teamwork exercise. Then he put on a video of horse use in the park, especially concerning environmental sensitivity in the back-country. When there was a mention in the film about how nice some of the old equipment was, but that the new equipment was lighter and so more environmentally friendly, Gord quipped that with "environment" out and "heritage" in, maybe the film would now have to be redone to favour the older, heavier equipment! Gord was the producer of the film, a project left over from when he was a back-country supervisor, and this was a rough first cut that he had to review. The film was being made to send to people applying for permits to ride in the park.

That ended at 2:30 p.m., and it was back to the computer, sending detailed written comments on the film. Then Gord went through the paper mail, reviewing mostly routine things that had to be signed, budget documents and time sheets. Someone went by and Gord asked "Glen, were you guys out after that bear this afternoon?" No, Glen had been experimenting with a new tranquilizer dart, and he told Gord about the optimal distance to shoot one into a elk (twenty-two yards) and what the size of the syringe should be. "We could do a big bull with one dart."

Glen left at 3:10 p.m., and it was back to the mail: a couple of visitor complaints about traffic, about wildlife, and about a logging truck that pushed a sheep off the road. They were addressed to Charlie Zinkan and had been forwarded to Gord. A memo came from accounting about the cost of refilling the oxygen bottles used in first-aid and rescue. A call for papers for a geographical information system conference was forwarded by Gord to other people. All the while, the park's radio was playing in the background, and the dispatcher nearby in the building had just handled a call concerning an accident on the road. There was also a series of bulk items for information, including one on guidelines about a "bear management" plan.

At 3:55 p.m., Gord heard his name on the radio, and someone came to ask if he was available to talk to two climbers. So Gord went out to the front desk and met a couple of Australians who needed advice about climbing a particular peak. Gord knew the routes well. When they left, two other men presented themselves, having returned from the back-country and told Gord about the condition of the trails.

At this point, Gord informed me that he had planned to do a boat ride on the river to look for a dead body but that it was now too late in the day to go. Some days earlier, a visitor got drunk and persuaded someone else to go over Bow Falls in a raft with him. No one had ever done so successfully. At the last minute, the other fellow jumped clear, but the first one disappeared. The initial search was unsuccessful; it could take several days for a drowned body to float to the surface.

On other such days, Gord said he would spend more time talking to supervisors. But on weekends there were fewer calls for information from staff people in the headquarters and regional offices, so it was easier to get his paperwork done. He also tended to have more committee meetings on weekdays. Gord said he tended to spend time on other days going out with the staff to patrol campgrounds, picnic areas and trailheads, chasing bears off the roads, talking to visitors, and just maintaining a park presence. For example, he said that on another day, he might have gone out to test the new darts. In a typical week, he said he might make two trips up to the headquarters administration building to discuss personnel or financial issues, and he spent a day a week at Lake Louise.

At 4:30 p.m., one of the staff members dropped in to discuss the rewording of a sign about firearm control at the entrance to the park and left shortly after.

It was at this point that Gord explained to me about the fifty-metre definition to distinguish his "product," as they called it, from that of his back-country colleague. So we began to talk about the edges, and he explained to me that his people had worked on the initial study of the parking lot, but the ski hill operator did not like it and so took it to the political level. Gord talked about the wide variety of concerns that had to be dealt with here – law enforcement, wildlife, public safety, forest fire management, etc. In effect, he and his colleagues were managing a full community, even if a rather peculiar one.

We chatted to 5:15 p.m., and on my way back to the centre of town, just a few minutes from Gord's office, I photographed elk grazing on the front lawns of private homes.

Managing Down

This was not a typical day, or, more to the point, it was typical of a quiet, in-house day. But even if only by suggestion and through discussion, this day also indicated quite clearly how close Gord was to the operations. This probably reflects two characteristics that are difficult to separate. One is that Gord had been in the job for only a few months and so retained some of his earlier operating activities, such as producing the film and doing mountain rescue. And the other is that this is first-line supervision, and so doing remains a natural and significant part of the job.

In fact, it would seem that the other managerial roles, like controlling, leading, communicating, even linking, revolved largely around doing. In other words, the focus seemed to have been on action more than on information or people per se. When discussing leading, for example, Gord described it as teamwork, with the leader very much a part of the operating team. Or, in the case of controlling, it seemed to take the form largely of the issuing of specific directives based on his knowledge of and involvement in the specific situation. The more formal aspects of controlling, especially regarding systems (such as budgets), seemed to reflect controls imposed on him that he in turn had to impose on the people in his unit.

Conceiving was not evident here this day, possibly because Gord was new in the job or perhaps because the frame was simply assumed: the park must be run and a myriad things must be done to maintain it, from finding a body in the river to making a film that explains good horseback-riding behaviour.

And again, the edges were evident, in fact here most sharply. Gord and his people are the ones who have to chase the bears away before they hurt the tourists or anger the truckers. Otherwise, people will battle with each other, "literally as well as figuratively," Gord added, and then the problems move from the tangible edges of the front-country operations to the political edges of park and regional administration.

Gord's frustration with some of the management jargon and procedures, those abstractions in contrast with his unit's actions, seems to reflect the nature of his job as well as his newness in it. His response to this strange phenomenon called "management" is captured nicely in Linda Hill's book *Becoming a Manager.*[19] In it she describes how she tracked for a year salespeople who had just become sales managers and the difficulties they encountered. Management in the formal sense, compared with Gord's view of leadership, must be a curious thing for anyone who has to cope with very tangible operating problems and doubly curious when first encountered, especially in a mountain park. It suggests that organizations should give special attention to the training of new managers, something all too rare today.

What perhaps magnifies this frustration is the nature of the edge on which Gord, or any other front-line supervisor, sat. He found himself between the operations and the administration.

On one side were all the tangible problems of managing this natural setting, including the host of naturally occurring edges there – between the truckers and the tourists, the residents and the elk, even the elk and the bears. Of course, except for the last, these are not really "natural" at all, but rather occur by virtue of our imposition as human beings on our "natural" environment. Indeed, the very phrase "managing the natural setting" has to be a kind of oxymoron: that setting managed itself just fine for millennia without our "management." Now we have "bear management plans"!

And on the other side were the abstractions of administration as well as the peculiarities of politics, which themselves formed an edge, hence Gord's frustration in finding the promises of "decentralization" and "empowerment" usurped by the political manœuvring.

The truly natural edges, such as between the elk and the bear, elicit the tangible people-imposed edges, such as between the bears and the tourists and, in turn, between the tourists and the truckers, which in turn elicit the more abstract political edges, such as between the ski hill operators and the environmentalists. As this happens, the issues become more pervasive and more ideological, and they leave the domain of Gord's operations, which actually left him caught in the middle. And thus we found his response to this strange work called management.

We believe we have developed all kinds of fancy procedures to manage things, yet we have barely begun to come to grips with these kinds of problems – real problems, in real operations. Our procedures work wonderfully well in the administrative offices, where we rearrange boxes on charts (for example, Parks reporting to Heritage, whatever that means, instead of Environment), and formulate all kinds of well-intentioned plans that have little to do with the elk and darts of daily life. There, too many of these procedures seem to be quaint at best, counterproductive at worst. And so the managers are left to manage in a vacuum.

Of course, all of these edges are really mirror images of the same thing, all of them contrived in one way or another. People establish themselves in a natural setting in such a way that an animal ambling into a valley, or even drawn to it for the convenience of finding food, becomes an imposition. And the more people come, and the greedier their demands, the more these problems magnify, and so the more "political" the whole situation becomes. Politics, of course, is the way we fight with each other figuratively, over our self-assumed right to "manage" the natural environment.

A MODEL OF THE EDGES

Edges abound in the management of Parks Canada. Edges, of course, abound everywhere, if you want to see them. But here you cannot possibly miss them. The three managers I observed all dealt with some of the same edges. After all, that parking lot came up in all their work. But they dealt with them differently, on different levels of abstraction, and these various issues tended to manifest themselves in different sorts of edges.

As shown in Figure 2.2, in the terms of conventional hierarchy, with ground at the base and government at the top, or the parks at the bottom and the politicians at the top, Gord especially managed the edge between the operations and administration, which can be referred to as the operating edge and is shown horizontally across the bottom of the figure. He connected action to administration. Charlie's was especially the stakeholder edge, shown vertically to either side of him, as various outside players brought tangible pressures to bear especially on him. He connected influence to programs. And Sandy's job was to manage especially on the political edge, shown horizontally above her, particularly between

Figure 2.2 *A Model of Managing on the Edges*

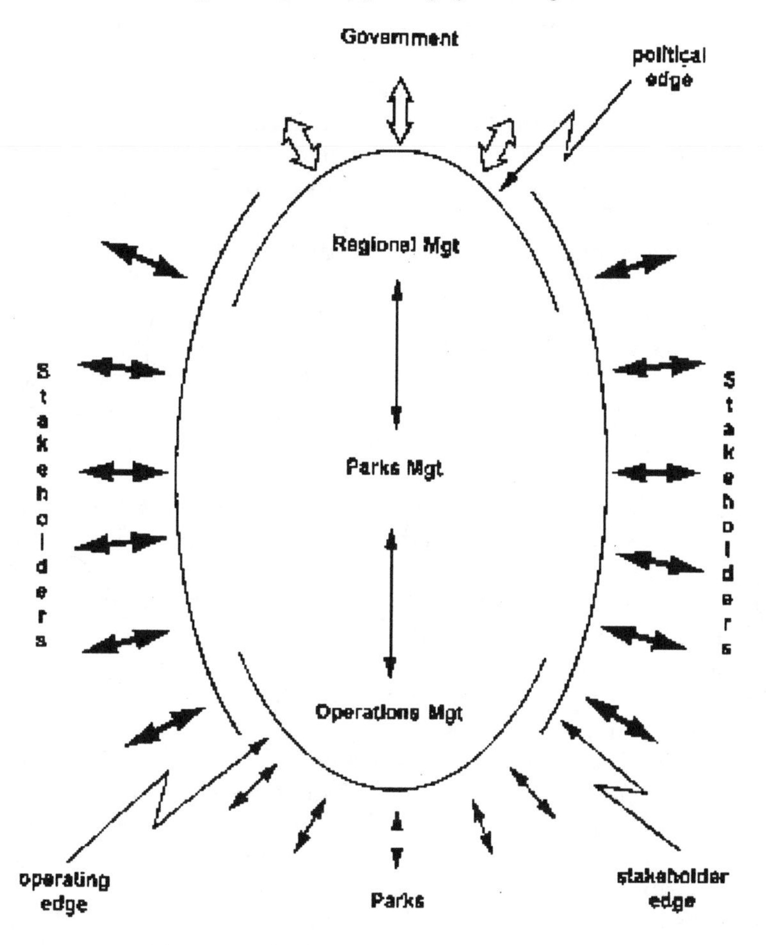

the authorities and politicians in Ottawa and the parks in western Canada. She connected politics to process.

As one "moves up" this hierarchy, which in reality is really down off the mountains, into the plains, and then on to the low country of the east where the capital is found, as the horizontal operating edge gets turned into vertical stakeholder edges and then into the horizontal edge of politics, the issues get more abstract and less nuanced as the positions get blunter and more symbolic. And so the system gets tied increasingly into knots, and cohesive management becomes all that more difficult to effect.

This is not to imply that any one of these three managers was free of the edges faced by the other two. That is why the lines have been rounded on the figure. Gord and Sandy clearly received stakeholder influences too, while Charlie and Sandy had to face some of the operating issues, and Gord and Charlie felt some of the political pressures. But there did seem to be this difference in focus, manifested especially in the nature of these three jobs. Gord seemed to be largely a doer, who led, controlled and linked in terms of action. Charlie seemed to be largely a linker outwards, a mediator between the different members of the park's community. And Sandy seemed to be mainly a linker upwards, to the political context of Ottawa, whose concerns she conveyed back into the system, especially in the role of controller.

Each of them was a manager in his or her own right. Yet, each could also be placed in different spots on the concentric circles of our model, in a sense sharing the same management process. If Gord managed especially downwards, from the outer circle of action, then Charlie managed especially outwards, from the middle circle of people, while Sandy managed especially upwards, from the inner circle of information. In these respects, Gord knew the details best, Charlie the pressures best, Sandy the politics best. Somehow, together they had to factor all this into a coherent decision-making process. How they did so – indeed whether they really did so – remains a mystery. Certainly the planning systems do not explain it. This may have helped, or perhaps they just represented some kind of rite,[20] another of those things that had to be done in the hope that something would work or else that at least something was being done.

Charlie was in the middle of all this, not just in our diagram, and so he was perhaps the one who got hit the hardest by the political forces, with little place to hide. Sandy, in contrast, had her escape route to the power structure of Ottawa, while Gord had his into the operations of the park. But Charlie was pulled both ways, as well as pushed from all sides, with no obvious place to go.

There is a great advantage in being able to manage something as real and beautiful as a mountain park. People care, they are naturally motivated. There is much to do and a wonderful setting within which to do it. The trouble is that people get motivated about different things, and they sometimes care too much. There remains that "discontinuous mandate of protection and preservation." Planning documents can articulate lofty ideals, which, as noted earlier, some people find helpful. But such documents can never specify the very difficult trade-offs that have to be managed constantly.

Many of the most interesting things, say the biologists, happen on they edges. That is where the living organisms encounter dynamic conditions that give rise to untold variety. But there is tension here as well, including competition with alien species. If you really want to see the edges, the real guts of government, coping with the impossible trade-offs of conflicting parties and alien species, then you would do well to get down on the ground where the elk graze on the front lawns and the truckers battle the tourists. Then maybe you can work "up" from there, to the abstractions of management that so mesmerize us, where people earn larger incomes ostensibly because their work is more important but perhaps really because they have to cope with all that much more nonsense, no small measure of it imposed by some of their own formalized systems. Supposedly necessary to deal with the complexities, perhaps all of this is really just a conceptual smokescreen for a species out of control, alien to its own environment. The bears know that the real problem is "people jams."

3

Managing Normatively

Policing is about control, in society, and that often converts into an obsession with direct control within the force. The Royal Canadian Mounted Police, on the three days I spent with them at least, appeared to be a different kind of force, one that controls more normatively than instrumentally, through culture rather than primarily by systems, rules and procedures. These days of observation, at these levels in the hierarchy – top, middle and bottom, the commissioner of the whole force, the commanding officer of H Division, Nova Scotia, and the commander of the New Minas (Nova Scotia) Detachment – revealed a kind of managerial work associated with normative controls.

In a hospital, where everything and everybody converges on one central point, namely the patient, a key factor for success is the ability to coordinate all the activity. But in a police force, the flow is exactly the opposite. All activities radiate out from the organization, into the community, in every possible direction. Indeed, this gets increasingly complex all the time as criminals become more clever. Thus a key factor for success becomes control – how to ensure that the dispersed forces all act in the best interests of the force and, of course, the public. Add to this the political component – the increasing sensibility of politicians to embarrassment by police actions, plus, in Canada, the vast geographical component, having to police the second-largest country in the world, ten million square kilometres of thinly populated territory, a great deal of it subjected to some of the harshest and most varied weather conditions anywhere – and you end up with a phenomenal problem of control. And, at the time of this observation, the RCMP employed 22,000 people.

But conventional administrative controls can be problematic. Budgets must certainly be used, and certain things have to be measured. But running the RCMP like a classical machine bureaucracy can be problematic:

the officers are normally well trained, and, once out on their own, especially in remote locations, they need to exercise considerable discretion without any real direct supervision. Thus, a case can be made for normative control, based on careful recruitment, followed by extensive indoctrination and socialization.

This seems to describe the RCMP. The force places great emphasis on the kinds of people it recruits and how its recruits are socialized. This is a form of control that dates back to the RCMP's legendary origins. It should be added here that while the RCMP acts as the police force in most of the provinces and many of the municipalities of the country, it does not do so in the most populous provinces (Quebec and Ontario) nor in any of the major cities, even those in the eight other provinces. These areas must be where the pressures of policing are the greatest and so too are the incentives to adopt more instrumental forms of control.

As we shall argue in conclusion, while instrumental control has hardly been absent in government, normative or cultural control has in some sense served as the glue that has held the whole system together. But recent years have taken a toll on the normative approach, beginning perhaps with the Planning, Programming, Budgeting System (PPBS), so popular in the 1960s, and accelerating more recently with all the paraphernalia associated with so-called "reinventing government" (citizens who magically become customers): the "bottom-line" managerialist approach, an emphasis on isolating units (the "executive agencies") and holding individual managers accountable for their performance, and especially doing everything possible to measure that performance.

These three days of observation in the RCMP suggest that we might well wish to consider a return to the days of balance, when pride in work, not just in managing it, and commitment to an institution, meant something special to people who really felt themselves to be "civil servants."

NORMAN D. INKSTER, COMMISSIONER, OTTAWA HEADQUARTERS, 4 MARCH 1993

I arrived at the complex of buildings that constitutes the headquarters of this veritable institution, in Ottawa, at 8:35 a.m. and was met at the door by superintendent David Cleveland, in uniform, who greeted me warmly. We went straight upstairs to the office of the commissioner, and, after a brief greeting, we went into an awaiting meeting.

Here, as during the rest of the day, most people were in uniform, the blaze of the yellow stripes on the pants most evident, with people senior in the hierarchy were always addressed formally ("Commissioner," "Deputy," "Sir," etc.). Their juniors were addressed by their first name, at least when it was known, which, in the commissioner's case, seemed to be rather often. During a later visit to the police college, he greeted the steward by first name, and in a session with the students from across the country he took a number of questions by first name also.

This reflected the nature of this highly respected chief executive, as well as the force that he managed. At the time, he was also serving a four-year term as head of Interpol. Few countries likely have a policeman as a national symbol (the "Mountie" dressed in red serge), and one might not have expected Canada to be among them. But perhaps it is one of the few countries that can afford to have such a symbol. Imagine a policeman symbolizing the United States! Certainly the head of Canada's federal police force reflected the nation's liberalism, in his personal demeanor and beliefs as well as in his managerial style, if not in the actual trappings of the office that surrounded him.

Commissioner Inkster was as relaxed as any manager I observed and very open on many of the contentious issues in policing today, including the acceptance of homosexuals on the force, marriages among the officers ("there were 125 of these," he told me with what sounded like a touch of pride), and even capital punishment. He believed in serious decentralization as well as honest communication within the force, and what I saw this day certainly supported this, particularly with regard to the promotion of "community-based policing." This means leaving wide latitude to the constables in the field and their detachment commanders, and, in turn, to the subdivision commanders and the commanding officers of the divisions, one for each province, who make up the entire line hierarchy in this organization.

This was an "inside day," according to the commissioner, and in part a somewhat ceremonial one – not coincidentally, presumably, given how much of this job, in the police work itself as well as dealings with ministers of the government, could be confidential and therefore closed to an outside observer. At no time during the day, however, did I get a sense that the commissioner or others were holding things back because of my presence. Moreover, ceremony is hardly an incidental part of this job. Overall, the sum total of the commissioner's activities observed, including the last two hours at his desk working on mail, with people dropping in, as well as the considerable time he allowed for my questions, left me with a broad sense of what it means to manage a large, complex police force, at least as Norman Inkster did so in the RCMP.

The 8:30 a.m. slot was dedicated to a regular meeting with the commissioner and his deputy commissioners, who manage the headquarters' units (operations, law enforcement and protective services, administration, and corporate management). Also present were the director of public affairs, Chief Superintendent Walker, Superintendent Cleveland, who served as the commissioner's executive officer, and the commissioner's executive assistant. Each took his turn to review the events of the last twenty-four hours and the actions that needed to be taken. Topics included stowaways on a ship that arrived in the Maritimes, protection for the prime minister during a speech in Toronto, security for party leaders in the upcoming election, and especially items in the press that mentioned the RCMP.

A packet of press clippings had been circulated, and at one point a clip was played from the CBC national news of the previous evening. It featured an interview with an ex-constable of East Indian extraction, in British Columbia, who had accused the force of prejudice, followed by a press conference with a number of other constables of minority groups who denied that such prejudice was prevalent in the force. It was clear from the reaction at this meeting that these constables had acted on their own initiative, which well illustrated the spirit of decentralization in the force.

Everyone was well prepared for the meeting, and the focus was on briefing each other, as well as acting to pre-empt possible negative consequences of events that, initially at least, were beyond the force's control. As Commissioner Inkster repeated several times during the day, he managed for "no surprises."

That meeting ended at 9:20 a.m., and the commissioner and deputy commissioners moved to another meeting room for their Senior Executive Committee meeting, which took place on an ad hoc basis, an average of twice a month. Here the agenda was highly structured, with formal presentations by other officers, followed by questions and discussion in order to secure formal top management approval of major items. At one point, Commissioner Inkster said of one item "I gather that we are prepared to approve ..."

The first item dealt with operating budgets, a second with a cost-recovery program, and a third with the acquisition of a jet airplane, considered a sensitive issue because, although the equipment was particularly needed in policing work such as in the case of moving dangerous criminals, getting security forces in place for prime ministerial speeches, etc., it could be seen otherwise. This last presentation was particularly detailed, with the commissioner highly informed about the details. Despite the formality of this particular presentation, the atmosphere in the room was rather relaxed, with no sense of rushing. Reference to the Treasury Board was made at a number of points, at this meeting and others, indicating both the influence of this central government budgeting agency and the commissioner's sensitivity to that influence. The meeting ended at 11:00 a.m.

We returned to the commissioner's office, where he turned to me for any questions. I was interested in the frustrations of practising necessarily abstract administration for someone who began as a constable. He mentioned that "the highly significant cases" do "make their ways through the headquarters," and that "on occasion," although "rarely," he could become involved in an investigation. He also discussed the decentralization, which he referred to as "a franchise approach": 700 detachments as independent franchises but controlled not by measurable indicators so much as by statements of expectations. In return, "the buzzword is no surprises: you are obliged to let us know" when something goes wrong.

But, he added, "you have to be in a position to make certain assumptions" when you empower others, otherwise there is the risk of being manipulated, and this has to do with an intimate understanding of the system being managed, however decentralized. Commissioner Inkster said that because of his thirty-six years on the force, including six years as commissioner, he knew all of the commanding officers personally. He also said he visited every division at least once a year and emphasized the need to "sit on the edge of the desk with your people" when doing so. Of particular importance to him was his belief that his people are "entitled to know why I make certain decisions," in effect to explain why the headquarters did what it did, to make its actions more visible.

We also discussed some of his more frequent outside contacts that I would not see this day: the solicitor general, once every two weeks on average, to whom he formally reported, as well as people in the minister's office to keep them informed; meetings with other ministers and deputy ministers; various government committees on which he sat (e.g., security); meetings with military people, foreign visitors including police officers and ambassadors, representatives of particular communities, such as native peoples, a bank president about credit card fraud, and so on.

At noon, we went to his car and were driven to the Canadian Police College, which trains officers of the force and of foreign forces as well; the RCMP has its main training facility for all new recruits in Regina, which the commissioner also visits regularly. He was there to lunch with and then address a class of about forty officers on this final day of their four-week program. An official photo with the class was followed by cocktails and lunch in the officers' mess. Lunch ended at 1:30 p.m. sharp, with the commissioner asking "Everybody done?" and in answer to a light-hearted "no" from the side, he replied "tough," and we all headed for a classroom.

There, after being introduced as a "visionary" leader, the commissioner spoke casually but seriously, without notes, for a half-hour, about the force and its needs in the future, exposing some very progressive views.

Then there began a long period of questions, some of them very blunt (e.g., about a "malaise" in one division), which were answered with equal bluntness. At one point, the commissioner discussed the experience the officers would need to move into various positions up the hierarchy, finishing with "And if you want my job, you don't need any of that!" Of course, the exact opposite was crystal clear to everyone who watched him perform in that room. Commissioner Inkster was clearly conveying information, but just as clearly he was conveying firm beliefs and instilling values about the culture of the RCMP. At 3:20 p.m., after the vigorous questioning died down, he said to the instructor "You wanted me to get out of here around three o'clock or so?" After he handed out the diplomas, we headed back to his office.

On the way, we discussed Interpol and the commissioner's concern, more as a kind of chairman of the board than as chief executive officer, with accomplishing a fairly major reorientation. He also emphasized again the importance of having the RCMP people understand the decisions that were made at headquarters and how he had set out to remove the mystery of the commissioner's office.

Back in the office at 3:45 p.m., the nature of activity changed significantly, as Commissioner Inkster turned to working with his executive assistant on scheduling, as well as to the mail on his desk, interrupted by telephone calls and requests for brief meetings. The deputies came in a number of times, briefly, on some more or less urgent matters, including possible consequences in Canada of the FBI arrest that day of an individual charged with bombing the New York World Trade Center, budget-cutting with regard to security at certain airports, a visit of two police officers from Zambia and how to accommodate their needs at the college, and some items of structuring and budgeting, including a fairly detailed discussion of costing police protection for designated protectees. Mostly, the commissioner was being informed during these meetings, but there were discussions about how to proceed as well, and, if he was not personally managing any of these issues, he did seem to remain close to their management.

A number of telephone calls also took place on the intercom concerning these issues, and there was also a call from one of the division commanders, with the commissioner commenting "Good for you" and "I'm in complete agreement with you," and from an affiliate about the research activity in the college.

The mail was varied: an internal report on tobacco smuggling, a document on a nominated candidate for the Order of Canada, a letter in support of a police officer in Israel, a letter from a coroner passed by a minister on what could have been a precedent-setting ruling, a memorandum about a terrorism response team, several requests to speak at or attend official meetings, and a request to approve the leave of absence of a commanding officer, "one of the few things we haven't formally delegated."

At about 6 p.m., Commissioner Inkster indicated that his work was winding down, and so I left, although he said he would stay until 6:30 to make a call to a police officer in Japan about changes to be proposed at an upcoming meeting of Interpol.

Policing the Culture

On the surface, this seems to be a job largely about control – about being informed of pending actions and granting approval, however formalized. But looked at more closely, that controlling was intimately wrapped up with leadership and in fact reflected a major concern with buffering. In effect, Commissioner Inkster could be seen as the guardian of an institution who worked hard at protecting its established culture.

Interestingly, he did this inside by allowing the RCMP to be more of what it had always been – a rather progressive and decentralized police force, originally because of the remoteness of its work (since it was founded to police the wild, remote, northwestern territories of Canada) but now because of current beliefs in empowerment. And so, while controlling internally seemed key, it was really leading the whole organization, with respect to protecting and enhancing the culture, that was key.

Commissioner Inkster commented at one point during the day that the highly disciplined, military-like structure made deciding on changes more difficult here, but once the decisions were made, the execution became that much easier. But surely the force's culture itself beyond these formalistic manifestations was a major factor in explaining the facilitation of change, as well as impediments to that change.

As noted earlier, culture is control here, and while every person socialized into the force helps to exercise that control, as was most evident in the press conference of those constables in British Columbia, it is its chief executive officer who must above all represent and uphold the culture. Norman Inkster most obviously did this with dedication and grace. To say that he was truly "on top of things" is thus to describe both his formal position in the hierarchy and his key role in sustaining the culture. Hence, in this job, the more obvious controlling blended into more subtle leading, with the latter appearing to emerge as the key role performed internally by the chief executive. He did "do," to be sure, helping to manage personally some of the more critical projects, and he certainly communicated, at length. But both seemed to stem from a pressing concern with leading in the cultural sense.

Looking outside as leader of an institution that has really become a legend, its chief executive has a major role to play in protecting and preserving its culture. That does not mean cutting it off from external influence, because this is what keeps it responsive, whether to shifting social norms or new policing technologies. It does not mean ensuring that such influence, transmitted inside, enhances its effectiveness.

The pressures on any police force today, and especially on its chief, have to be enormous. Outside influencers expect responsiveness to public demands, and governments expect directives to be turned automatically into formal controls. So the force can hardly act like a closed shop, in the service of its officers – even if there is no shortage of this behaviour in policing today. Norman Inkster appeared to understand and manage this, in both cerebral and insightful ways. He certainly knew the force intimately, and he seemed to work hard at dealing with those aspects of his job – namely the politics, the media, and today's social context in general – for which he could not have been trained.

So if linking was the key outside role here, it was practised not so much by representing influence out or transmitting influence in as by the subtle buffering between these two. Anticipated buffering was especially important here, for if the commissioner expected "no surprises" from his people, then he also preferred no surprises from outside circumstances either. Of course, policing means responding to unexpected events. But these do not have to be ones created by the police themselves! Thus, careful efforts seem to have been made, for example, to manage the fiscal controls of a Treasury Board and to avoid actions that could have led to embarrassment in the press. "I try to be a filter ... filter out the elements of panic, to sift out the emotion," was how the chief executive officer described his position at the interface.

How happy would an action-oriented police officer like Norman Inkster have been spending most of his time in the administrative and government offices of Ottawa? Even with, or perhaps especially with, the constant reminder of those uniforms? Rather happy, it seemed, because of Norman Inkster's pride in being able to protect an institution that was so important to him. This was a duty, to be sure, but so is policing itself.

In that regard, when I asked myself whether the frame of Norman Inkster's job was selected by himself or imposed on him by circumstances, I could not answer the question. The frame was very clear, as one watched him at work, and it had to do with maintaining the culture while adapting its practices. But its source was buried in thirty-six years of experience. In a truly effective institution, such as the Royal Canadian Mounted Police, when things go right, the leader reflects, enacts and embodies the system.

A.D.F. BURCHILL, COMMANDING OFFICER OF H DIVISION, HALIFAX, NOVA SCOTIA, 20 APRIL 1993

The operations of the RCMP are divided into divisions for each of the Canadian provinces. H Division covers Nova Scotia, one of the smaller provinces, with a population of 900,000, which has contracted with the force to provide its policing on the provincial level as well as in many of the smaller municipalities. As a result, this was not only a regional managerial job but also one that had a lateral but indirect reporting relationship, as indicated on the "organigram" (Figure 3.1) for H Division, which shows dotted lines to either side of the commanding officer, one to the attorney general of the province, the other to its solicitor general. This creates an interesting power relationship, because while the force has to be responsive to the provincial government, this is more of a contractual than a political obligation and so made it much easier to deflect potential political interference. Put differently, Commanding Officer A.D.F. (Allen) Burchill's line to the commissioner on that chart is not dotted!

Otherwise, the structure was quite straightforward: there were various technical services at the division headquarters: informatics, criminal operations, etc., and various administrative services like planning, while the operations throughout the province were divided into four subdivisions, which comprised fifty-two detachments in all, including twenty-one highway patrols, eight drug sections, five dog sections, etc.

C.O. Burchill's work, on this day at least, seemed to be quite straightforward as well. He suggested I come in at 7 a.m., but, in fact, he had been there since 6:35, reading a national and a local newspaper. There tend to be articles on the RCMP almost every day; in addition, there was to be an announcement that day of the RCMP decision to lay criminal charges in the very sensitive issue of a mine disaster that took place in Nova Scotia. Since he tried to keep his office open, especially early in the morning, he had me sit where I would not discourage visitors. That plus a note outside, since his secretary Ruby arrived only at about 8:30 a.m., did its job, since several of his branch officers soon dropped in.

At 7:15 a.m., the head of the Halifax subdivision, the largest of the four, with 284 people, came in. They discussed various issues, not making decisions so much as exchanging information casually. They spoke of rearrangements of the boundaries of two districts and its effects on municipal policing, appointments in the force, nomination for medals, and so on. This person left at 7:35 a.m., and after ten minutes more with the newspapers, the man in charge of criminal operations dropped in. There was "not much" to report, he said: a fatal car accident the night before; someone who had a gun but who shouldn't have; issues associ-

Figure 3.1 *Organizational Chart H Division (RCMP)*

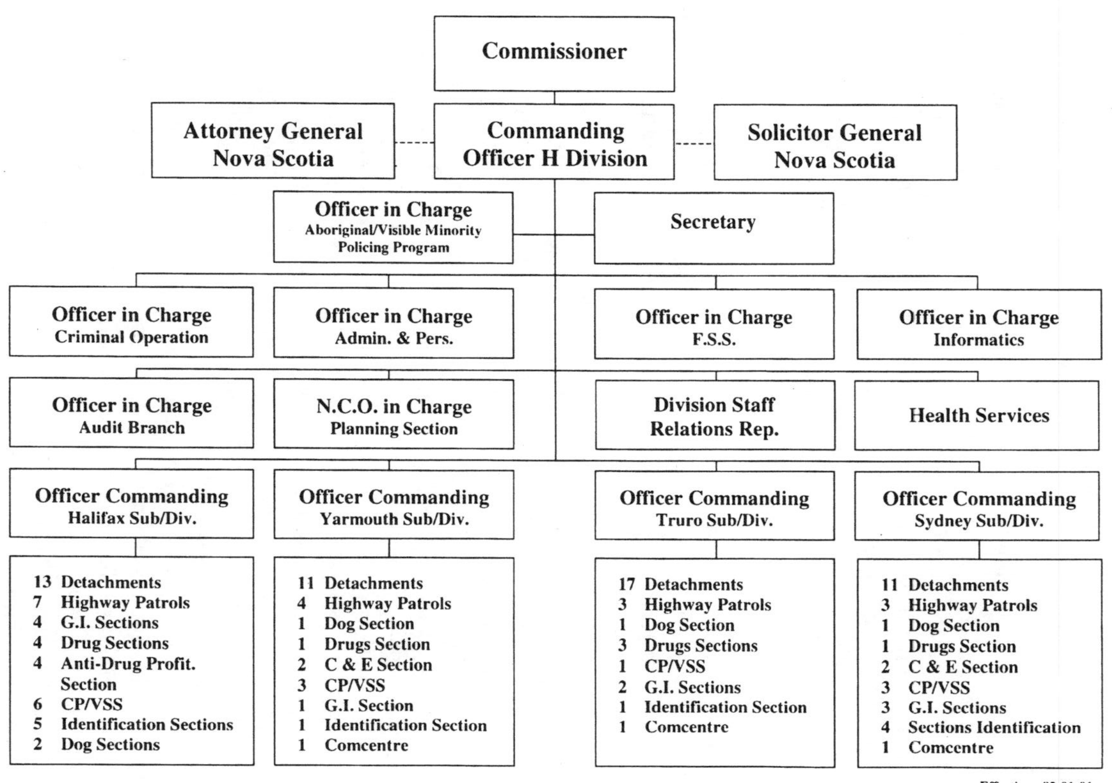

ated with the mine disaster press conference; and the transfer of certain people, which included discussion of people and events in the force across the country, an indication of how much this was one force from coast to coast. Mostly, information was exchanged, but in one case, on whether or not to lay charges, there was a request for authorization, which C.O. Burchill decided against. With an "Anyway, that's about it for this morning," this man left at 8:03 a.m.

He was immediately followed by the head of the audit section (audit of policing activities, not books), who came in with the comment, "I haven't seen you for a couple of weeks, so I thought I'd drop in to tell you what's going on." They discussed events in a small subdivision, an appointment for a fundraising drive, and the encouragement of, and resistance to, "bar walks" by the constables. He left at 8:17 a.m., and it was back to the newspapers until 8:30 a.m., when there were a couple of brief chats in the outer office. Then Ruby arrived, and they talked for a short time.

At 8:45 a.m., the deputy in charge of administration and personnel dropped in, the first person, besides Ruby, in civilian clothing. Again there was a steady stream of exchanged information, followed by "I don't really have much of anything else; got anything on your little list there?" and he left at 9:05 a.m.

Between the papers and the pile of messages on the desk, one item, concerning a new detachment for Nova Scotia, was looked at in detail to see if any of the changes made in the headquarters' review in Ottawa needed to be questioned. We chatted a bit too, especially about C.O. Burchill's relations with the provincial authorities. He met with them often, he said, but not this day, although a meeting with the Nova Scotia deputy minister of justice was scheduled for the next day, taking a preemptive position much in the spirit of the commissioner's motto of "no surprises." For example, he said that he tried to keep the provincial minister informed about problems so that he could handle questions in the legislature. He also remarked that in his dealings with the Ottawa headquarters, he generally worked through the deputies, only calling the commissioner if there was some kind of special problem.

At 9:35 a.m., a phone call came in from the organizer of the new 911 number in Halifax, explaining that the errors were fewer than thought earlier and mostly mechanical, in other words, not the fault of the force. In a few minutes, it was back to the mail, with Ruby coming in periodically, mostly to discuss scheduling. Most of the mail was from headquarters: "little drops of knowledge for the day," including a lengthy document on upcoming budget cuts. The commanding officer also took a lengthy telephone call, mostly listening with the comment near the end that "I knew about it the day it happened because I read about it in the newspaper," and, finally, "OK. That'll give me something to think about." This concerned a case where a judge questioned a witness's evidence, and the staff sergeant on the line was discussing his investigation of this and the possibilities of laying perjury charges.

At 10:15 a.m., we went downstairs to the "officers' mess" for coffee, where eight RCMP officers talked informally, about a gift for a "great supporter of ours," an officer who was quite ill, and a posting that was coming up out west.

Then, at 10:35 a.m., after a brief discussion outside the office about formal arrangements for the funeral of an officer who had just died, we headed into the management meeting, which took place every three or four weeks. "I'm informed," explained the commanding officer, "but this is a go-around-the-table to make sure they're informed." Fifteen people sat around a crowded table, one person elected by the staff, all the others representing specialized functions, with pictures of the Queen and the commissioner on the wall. They went over the minutes, then C.O. Burchill informed the group about several issues and, "with those comments," turned to the officer next to him to begin the go-around. The issues discussed ranged widely and included budget cuts, political events, intelligence on a racist group, labour relations, the coming press conference on the mine disaster, a new radio communication system being tested in H Division, tests for new recruits, succession planning and the movement of personnel. Most of this was straight informing, with each person presenting information on his own functional speciality. There was the occasional query, and a decision was taken to proceed on application of the new communication equipment, with C.O. Burchill commenting, "Well, I guess there's sufficient interest for a demonstration. I'll let you decide on the time."

The meeting ended at 12:15 p.m., and, after C.O. Burchill asked one officer into his office for a couple of minutes to give Burchill comments on a document the officer had read, asking for "nothing too long, a page and a half would be about right," we headed off to lunch. Sandwiches were bought in the canteen and eaten in the officers' mess, with three or four other people. One issue discussed was the press conference, with Burchill commenting, "I just wanted to be there to show I'm interested."

Back in the office at 1:00 p.m., between the occasional person dropping in briefly, in a couple of cases to pick up a document that had to be reviewed by the commanding officer before being released externally, plus a telephone call from the Nova Scotia Department of Justice about replacing an RCMP officer who had been seconded there, it was back to the mail: certifying signatures on outgoing documents, a letter from the Department of National Defence about a criminal investigation, and an invitation to a "Good Neighbours" program.

At 2:00 p.m., C.O. Burchill went into a meeting about the "car computers" that were being tested in H Division. An information technology team of three people from the headquarters in Ottawa had been there for several weeks doing a field evaluation and they were reporting to ten people assembled from the division. After the report, C.O. Burchill commented, "It's one of the few things that's really improved policing operations in the last twenty-five years. It's unfortunate we've worked all that time developing systems for managers" when it should have been for the operators. He also noted how receptive the constables had been to the new system. Others made various comments, and the meeting ended at 2:22 p.m.

Asked how he knew the response of the constables to equipment in their cars when his own job was so removed from them, C.O. Burchill said, "I get out to detachments." He said he tried to visit all fifty-two once a year but felt the reality was probably closer to every eighteen months. There he preferred to sit in the coffee room with the constables and talk, and he noted, consistent with the observation of these other two days, that RCMP people are rather outspoken, more than in "my day."

Then, for most of the rest of the afternoon, aside from a coffee break in the officers' mess, it was back to the mail, with the occasional telephone call or someone dropping in. Of the mail, there was the following: a notice from the St. John's Ambulance about a board meeting; an invitation to a police golf tournament; some information for perusal on a reorganization of informatics; a performance evaluation to review, which he dropped off in a branch officer's office; a memorandum from the police chiefs' association about armour-piercing bullets; a letter from a member of the provincial legislative assembly about someone not getting his share of local RCMP towing service, which was forwarded to the detachment in question; a congratulation letter to sign for someone promoted to a government job; circulars of post-retirement job possibilities; an invitation to a spring ball in a subdivision (some such thing "almost every weekend," such as a university convocation: "A lot of things are just traditional ... I enjoy it; my wife does it for the cause"); a grievance from a retiring officer about the insurance not covering a hearing aid, sent back to the grievance committee in the belief that they should make a recommendation; a Canadian law enforcement magazine; a press release on the charges laid in the mine disaster, which he read carefully and then took to the criminal operations officer's office; a unit's request for an additional staff slot (which was refused); and a planning document sent for his approval, which was granted.

Twice, branch officers dropped in briefly to have letters signed, and there were three telephone calls, one to the wife of the staff sergeant who just died to express condolences, a second from a friend at headquarters in Ottawa to commiserate about the reorganization of his branch, and possibly to fish for a new job in Nova Scotia, and a third about arrangements for the staff sergeant's funeral.

At 5:30 p.m., C.O. Burchill left the office, offering to drop me off in town (Halifax), so that we had a last chance to discuss his job in the car. On the lateral nature of his communication, he said, "When the [provincial] minister calls, he calls the C.O." A particularly interesting case recently was the RCMP reaction to the blocking of roads near an Indian reserve in New Brunswick. As extra forces were needed, some had to be sent from Nova Scotia. Here, however, the call went from the provincial government via Ottawa headquarters to him who passed it to the people who could take the action. In general, he saw himself as having to keep two sets of people happy, his own headquarters and the provincial government. But it seemed clear that the authority flowed to one, with the other more in a client relationship.

C.O. Burchill admitted that there was more immediate satisfaction being a constable but that in his job you "can feel good for what your own people do." He felt he had considerable autonomy, "a good bit of room to move," with few directives from his boss, the commissioner who had earlier described this relationship in much the same way.

Maintaining the Information Flow

The remarkable thing about this day was the proportion of time devoted to communicating. This particular day might have been especially focused in this regard (an outside observer would logically be invited in for a mostly "inside day," and perhaps a relatively quite one at that). But so much of the mail and so many of the contacts had to do with informing and especially being informed that it is difficult to imagine this not being a central part of this job. When I suggested this to C.O. Burchill, he said, "That seems to be about my job."

C.O. Burchill sat in the hierarchy between the headquarters that sets much of the policy, establishes most of the systems, and influences many of the norms and the detachments of the highly trained and very much empowered constables who carry out the policing work. So the controlling role, especially with regard to the issuing of specific directions, did not seem to loom very large here – despite all the trappings of hierarchy and titles.

Again, this is a cooperative system in which the people, who have duly imbibed the culture, know what they have to do and do it. This was evident in the Halifax officers' mess, where the conversation seemed as likely to be about some appointment in Alberta or some event in the Arctic as about a crime in Nova Scotia. But it was no less evident in conversation with a constable who came to Nova Scotia from embassy duty in Ottawa and hoped to go next to Quebec to perfect her French. Communication, in other words, is "inside" the unit being managed, but also very significantly "within" the rest of the organization, as opposed to "outside" of the RCMP. Just how effective this is, among 22,000 people spread across 10,000,000 square kilometres of territory, was perhaps best illustrated by the story of an applicant for the force who was accused of cheating on an entrance examination in Central Canada as a result of allegedly having been assisted by a member in the High Arctic.

Where does that leave the commanding officer of a division? When all runs as it is supposed to, in the spirit of the commissioner's "no surprises," and, in this day at least that seemed to be the case, then the answer seems to be: not with a great deal of pressure. And so the job seemed to be largely one of facilitating the information flow, keeping things humming, on track – to evoke all the common metaphors. The commanding officer linked the headquarters to the detachments by ensuring that both were informed by him, as well as he informed from them, to ensure no surprises, or at least to be able to act when one did occur. Policing can involve any exceptional event in society, so managers of police forces have to be very broadly and thoroughly informed. The most obvious example of this, given his distance from actual policing, was the commanding officer's understanding of the computers in the patrol cars and how the constables were reacting to them, an impression confirmed in discussion with a highway patrol constable the next day.

I saw little controlling this day, and almost all of it was the formal authorization of letters, reports, procedures and actions of an officially designated nature, often in the process of flowing up or down the hierarchy. In effect, this controlling dealt with the certification of particular things designated for this level of the hierarchy. On the occasions where an ad hoc decision had to be made, for example, to proceed on something, I had less the sense of personal choice than of natural consensus.

There was more controlling than this, in fact, but much of it seemed concerned with systems or arrangements that flowed right past the commanding officer. There was, for example, the "audit branch," which audited policing, not budgets. A member of this branch might sit in a police car with a constable: "After four hours, you find out if they like their managers or not!" Or the audit person might encourage the constables to do "bar walks." In sharp contrast, when the Office of the Auditor General of Canada, years ago, had difficulty doing its "comprehensive audits," assessing "value for money," because of the difficulties of measuring so much of what counts in government, it reverted to checking off a list of best management practice, such as engaging in formal planning, as a surrogate for performance!

If most of the job this day involved communicating, with some controlling at the informational level, then what of the other roles? Focused leading was not particularly in evidence. There was certainly an affective side to the commanding officer's contacts with subordinates, but this is normal in any managerial job. The interpersonal relationships seemed to be clearly established, and stable, as seemed to be the structure of the operating teams. Although people come and go, in this situation, they all come from the same culture. Culture-building, however, was not in special evidence here, although the presence of a strong culture, and C.O. Burchill's role in supporting it, certainly was. There was considerable attention to staffing and appointments, as well as to performance evaluating, but this seemed to have more to do with systems of control than with leading per se.

I saw little doing or dealing that day, although there must have been a certain amount of negotiating with the provincial authorities in this job but in line with the established culture. So when a provincial government complains about police reluctance to get tough with strikers, for example, the commanding officer can hold the line by evoking RCMP attitudes about dealing with such issues.

Some linking was evident in telephone calls and in the mail, and clearly there had to be much more of this than I saw this day. The commanding officer of any RCMP division may communicate mostly up and down a formal hierarchy, but there are also the lateral links to the provincial government, a kind of long-term client. Yet, the political dimension of this, as noted, appeared to be muted by the strength of the RCMP hierarchy, although, I suspect, the delicacy of dealing with this is not to be underestimated. Likewise, given the commonality of dealing with the different provincial governments, the conceiving role, and strategy formation in particular, would not appear to be paramount in this job. Of course, there are important decisions to be made concerning these relationships, but perhaps more within existing strategies than to create new ones. Figure 3.2 depicts the various flows of communication around this managerial job.

One can distinguish "natural" from "unnatural" managerial jobs. The former deal with self-standing organizational units, a hospital, for exam-

Figure 3.2 *Flows of Communication in the RCMP Divisional Commanding Officer's Job*

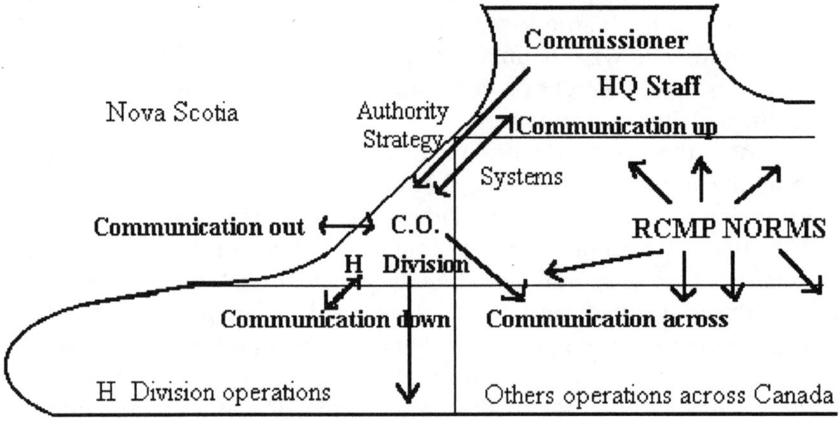

ple, or a privately owned corporation. The latter are often created artificially to cut spans of control – the sales manager for Asia Pacific in that corporation, for example, or the head of three or four nursing units in that hospital. Is H Division a natural managerial unit? Yes and no, seems to be the right answer. Nova Scotia is a natural entity, a distinct province with its own legislature, courts, newspapers, etc., not to mention geography (although a glance at the borders of Saskatchewan, all straight lines, might cause one to question the "naturalness" of some of the Canadian provinces). And so, having to liaise with the province seems to be natural managerial work.

But given the strength of the RCMP at top and bottom, the culture of systems emanating from the headquarters, and the professionalism and empowerment of the police officers themselves, this job also exists to cut the spans of control from one end of the hierarchy to the other. In that sense, it is not entirely natural, which may explain why I did not get a sense of a hectic pace here or of a lot of pressure or of critical strategizing. Things seemed to be well organized and mostly smooth flowing in this unit of about a thousand people, in contrast, say, to the swirling of activity I observed around the head of a hospital or the frenetic pace of the president of a small retail chain.

Yet, there is another side to this too. The incumbent was deeply involved; he seemed to understand fully the culture of the overall organization and to have a deep appreciation for its basic operations at the ground level. So he could help to hold the two together and keep the information flowing between them. And that is a most natural way to manage!

STAFF SERGEANT R.G. HUMBLE, COMMANDER OF THE NEW MINAS (NOVA SCOTIA) DETACHMENT, 20 APRIL L993

This was not the kind of day I expected. My intention was to observe management at the three main levels of the RCMP hierarchy: the commissioner, a division commanding officer, and a detachment commanding officer. But somehow we got our signals crossed, and Staff Sergeant R.G. (Ralph) Humble had more or less set aside his time to accommodate me, namely to discuss his job and the detachment. This may have been just as well, since much of his work that I did see involved interacting with people coming and going in the main office, and my presence may have been obtrusive. In any event, besides partially observing a manager at work, I undertook to interview one as well and so learned some other kinds of things.

Commander Humble had been with the RCMP for thirty-four years, the last five as head of the detachment in the small town of New Minas in Nova Scotia's pretty, rural Annapolis Valley, covering a population of 45,000. He was, in fact, due to retire in a few days, to take up a job with the court down the street. They ran three "watches" (shifts) here during the day (eight hours) and night (nine hours), with a few hours in the middle of the night being not covered (5 to 7 a.m.). As well, there was a highway patrol and a Forensic Identification Section with three full-time people that also served two other detachments. The staff numbered thirty-eight in all, including "civilians." To put things into perspective, when Los Angeles put all of its available forces on the street in anticipation of the verdict in the second police trial about the Rodney King beating, the number of murders that day went down by about as many as in all of Nova Scotia (with about a quarter the population) in a whole year!

"In Halifax," Staff Sergeant Humble said, referring to the division headquarters, "just as long as those numbers are filled in," implying everything else was OK. There were, indeed, a lot of numbers. He handed me a sheet listing twenty-one "review items" that he either submitted himself or else reviewed, ranging from annual assessments to search warrants, a prisoner activity book, detachment work plans, to budget review, and diary dates. "Of course, our concern is having a name besides the number." And when something serious like a murder took place, the need for a stake-out, even just the arrival at the station of several suspects for interviewing all at once, then the place could take on a sense of urgency. "You see it all," he said.

In my day with a hospital head nurse, I described a craft style of management, as opposed to a boss or a professional style, which combines involvement with empowerment and a good deal of managing in the open, on one's feet. I heard much of this here too, and observed it as well a number of times during the day. "You can't know it if you haven't done it," Staff Sergeant Humble said, but he also added "I have to know enough to have members respect me, yet not get in too deep ... to have pride, you have to have responsibility. What I try to instil is, 'If you do it, I'll support you.'" In contrast, he felt the levels above him were becoming top heavy, with people who were purely administrative, such as policy people or researchers who did not always have to make the split-second decisions. At the base, he felt, managers had to know everything: "They couldn't afford to be specialists."

There was a steady buzz of conversation from the outer office, a large open area with many windows and a number of desks, where the constables sat as they came from and went out on their patrols. But the pace was much more calm than the one I observed, for example, in the nursing station of the hospital, perhaps because while both did their paperwork in this central place, the nurses did their operating work nearby whereas the constables dispersed far and wide to do their operating work. Moreover, and perhaps of greater importance, there seemed to be much less need for coordination among the different kinds of work being done here, and so the buzz was perhaps more social than informational.

At one end, behind glass, to isolate the noise, was the communications centre, in touch with all the cars and rapid access to electronic files across the country. To Staff Sergeant Humble, "This is really the beehive of activity." That faced the front door, which opened into a protected area, behind glass that was carefully sealed. Elsewhere in the building was a garage, which opened straight into several cells, a bank of interview rooms, a number of sealed rooms to hold evidence, and a breathalyzer-test room. The forensic laboratories were upstairs.

Between our conversations, staff officers came in to get things signed, which seemed to be mostly a formality. Many of these were operating reports, but all financial bills (e.g., all legal fees) had to be signed by the commanding officer as well, after being verified by the clerical staff. Periodically, Staff Sergeant Humble would go into the main office "just to talk to the boys," although five of the constables were female, a change in recent years that he felt "works well," especially concerning disturbances and sexual assault investigations, where he felt women officers performed more effectively.

Then someone came in, a plain clothes investigator, and handed Humble what seemed to be a fair amount of money, for which a form was signed. "It's a cash business," he said with seriousness. The money was for informants, mostly concerning drugs (but also stolen property), who are actually asked to receipt and even sign for it. Staff Sergeant Humble took out a calculator "to balance the accounts" and then put the money in a safe, stopping again to chat in the general office.

Someone then dropped a file off about an armed robbery in a credit union. Every file has to be reviewed by someone of higher rank, I was told. But part of the job too, he said, is to keep up-to-date on statistical information, to see the patterns in crimes. So there was a kind of yin and yang between the specific reports and the aggregated figures.

A call came in from a fellow detachment commander elsewhere in the province. They talked about his retirement and, common in many RCMP conversations, about the training of recruits and the transferring of people into new positions. Staff Sergeant Humble urged his caller to accept a proposed transfer: "You'll benefit from it in the long run." Another call followed about where to put some crime prevention materials that were being delivered.

It was now 11:15 a.m. I had been there since 8:30 a.m., talking to Staff Sergeant Humble in between the signing and the phone calls and chats in the main office. I felt my presence was becoming more obtrusive, since he seemed to want to spend more time in the outer office but was reluctant to do so. So when he asked if I would like to go out in a highway patrol car, I accepted gladly. I was introduced to Constable Dianne Stairs, and, as we left, Staff Sergeant Humble was out in the main office, checking with a repairman about a machine.

No schedule was established for this time in the car – when Constable Stairs asked how much time I had, I said "Let's just go and see." We went for almost four hours, and I was able to see the RCMP from yet another angle, that of the constable out in the world. This was not about management per se, except indirectly, but I was able to take advantage of the experience to write a short story, which speaks for itself. ("An Ordinary 'Watch' for the Extraordinary," published in the RCMP magazine, *Pony Express* July/August 1994.) I would like to add here that the professionalism, empowerment and dedication of the force was amply demonstrated in this experience. Once in that car – mostly the constables work alone here – she seemed to be a rather autonomous entity, although, of course, that autonomy was deeply rooted in the training and the systems that tie the constables to the force, not to mention the radio that serves as an umbilical cord back to the detachment and on to the rest of the country.

When I returned at 3 p.m. after a quick lunch next door, Constable Stairs was in Staff Sergeant Humble's office explaining her experience in a bordering province where officers were called to deal with the blocking of a road by a native band. She had been in full riot gear for ten hours. Staff Sergeant Humble had called her in because, on looking over her expense account, he could find no claim for lunch. It turned out to have been free.

In the time I was gone, there had been a sudden death of a sick woman down the road. Staff Sergeant Humble had to send an officer there but also went over to make sure it was being properly looked after. He also had a prescheduled visit with an investigator of a series of robberies, to meet some of the people involved, etc., and a meeting with some local people who had made a complaint that led to an investigation. They wanted his update on it, which he saw as a kind of public-relations gesture.

While I was there, Staff Sergeant Humble went over the file on a sexual assault charge, to decide whether the victim, who had since moved to Ontario, would be a good enough witness to bring back to testify since, otherwise, they would not be able to lay charges. He was also in and out of his office a lot. He tried to touch base with every member of the evening shift, he said, especially if they had been off for a few days, or on night watch, and so when he heard different ones arriving, he would go out to meet them. He also tried to drop by at night from time to time, he said, to "make sure they know I'm interested in what they're doing."

He talked about being available to give advice and guidance, based on his experience, and agreed with my observation that there appeared to be little in the way of him giving direct orders or instructions. Every couple of months, however, he said he was in the habit of holding a meeting with all the members of the detachment to discuss his goals and those of the division commanding officer as well as the commissioner. To Staff Sergeant Humble, being an effective manager meant being a good and sympathetic listener.

"I don't have a lot of contact with Halifax," he said. "Sure, if I have a problem I know who to call," but "I don't talk to headquarters more than I have to," mostly about things that were needed, such as new equipment. This sentiment was expressed on the other end too, because Commanding Officer Burchill in Halifax, when he explained with whom he had arranged this day for me, said "He must be doing well; I seldom hear from him."

Connecting Empowered Professionals

It is difficult to believe that this job is as calm and organized as it seemed that day, and, surely, had I been a more effective fly on the wall, I would have seen things differently. But just as surely, Staff Sergeant Humble was not masking some kind of frenetic job either. Things are highly organized in the RCMP, between the formalized systems on one end and the empowered professionals on the other. Here, as at the two other levels in the hierarchy, and even more evidently with the highway patrol officer, the commissioner's motto of "no surprises" seemed to be very much in evidence.

A detachment commander maintains the flow of authority between control and professionalism. But by being at the base level, instead of in a divisional headquarters, where the flow of communication seemed key, or at Ottawa headquarters, where the maintenance of the culture seemed to be key, a kind of low-key leading appeared to be central here. This helps to sustain the morale and well-being of the "members," as Staff Sergeant Humble referred to the operating staff, while they go about doing their work with relatively little need for direct supervision. This leading seemed to be mostly the one-on-one kind and included mentoring, coaching, supporting, advising, and the like. Maintaining the overall culture was clearly evident too, but not as much as in the job of the commissioner, who has to deal with the force at large (for example, in publications or speeches). Likewise, there seemed to be a team-building aspect to the leadership here too, but because people work in good part individually (as in going out alone on highway patrols), again this seemed less important than the one-on-one leading.

There was evidently a good deal of control in this job too, as elsewhere in the force. But surprisingly little of that seemed to be control downward, into the detachment. Most of it was control upward (satisfying the various overall RCMP systems and procedures, by filling out various forms and formally, almost ritualistically, authorizing various decisions). What this implies is not the controlling role of the manager (i.e., into the unit) but, in fact, the linking role of the unit to the overall system. The main aspects of the manager's controlling role, making directive choices for others in the unit, developing systems for the unit, and designing its overall structure, were not greatly in evidence, in what I saw or in what Staff Sergeant Humble discussed, although there had to be some of that in this job too. Thus, when at one point I described Staff Sergeant Humble's job to him as appearing to be on the edge of leading and communicating, but not controlling, he replied "I would say you're right on the money." He agreed with me that his job involved more guidance and advice than giving orders and instructions.

Being at the base level of management naturally involved a certain amount of doing too, especially filling in for others and, perhaps more on the edge between controlling and doing, getting involved in specific investigations, etc. to ensure they were proceeding correctly. But his visit this day to the people in the community to update them on an investigation, seemingly the role of dealing or at least communicating, is perhaps better described as linking, given his depiction of it as a public relations activity. Linking is, of course, an important role also, since the detachment commander represents the RCMP in the local community, much as the division commanding officer represents it to the province. But, again, linking would seem to be a rather straightforward role and perhaps not as important as that of leading.

The frame of this job seemed clear enough at this level and was probably rather stable. It was largely imposed by the overall system, probably more in fact by the overall culture than by any specific, intended strategies that came down the hierarchy. Staff Sergeant Humble, of course, put his own personal stamp on this.

The comparison of a police station with a hospital ward is interesting, because both do rather professional and sensitive work. As noted earlier, whereas the problem in the hospital is to coordinate all the different specialists who converge on the individual patient, the problem in the police force is to control the various specialists who disperse individually to the world at large. That probably makes the job of head nurse, at the base level, far more interactive than this one, at least as I observed someone there involved in more decision-making and team-building in a much more hectic job. Control in the police, at least in a force as well organized as the RCMP, is built largely into the systems, procedures and norms so that the controlling role of the police manager at the base would seem to be diminished in favour of other roles, especially leading and linking. In that sense, a detachment commander like Ralph Humble sits between the professionals who know what they have to do and the higher authorities who know how they want to control them; his job is to make sure this connection is smooth.

The Policing Culture

A clear message emerges from these three days, reinforced right up and down this sharply delineated hierarchy. While control is critical in the highly dispersed work of policing, and traditional controls clearly abound in the RCMP, what really seems to matter in this force is the use of culture (normative control) to keep everything running on track. It appeared on these three days to be defined and especially reinforced at the senior level, to be communicated down and up the hierarchy by the middle level, and to be reinforced with leadership at the base level.

If so, then hierarchy may not quite be the best way to describe this organization. Perhaps the senior managers are better described as being "at the centre" rather than "at the top." As drawn in Figure 3.3, the force can thus be shown as a disk, with the detachments or stations, as segments, radiating out in all directions. Within each can be found records, administration and custody on the inside, flowing out to communications, patrol and investigations at the edges, and then on to the community all around.

Figure 3.3 *Police Department Organigraph*

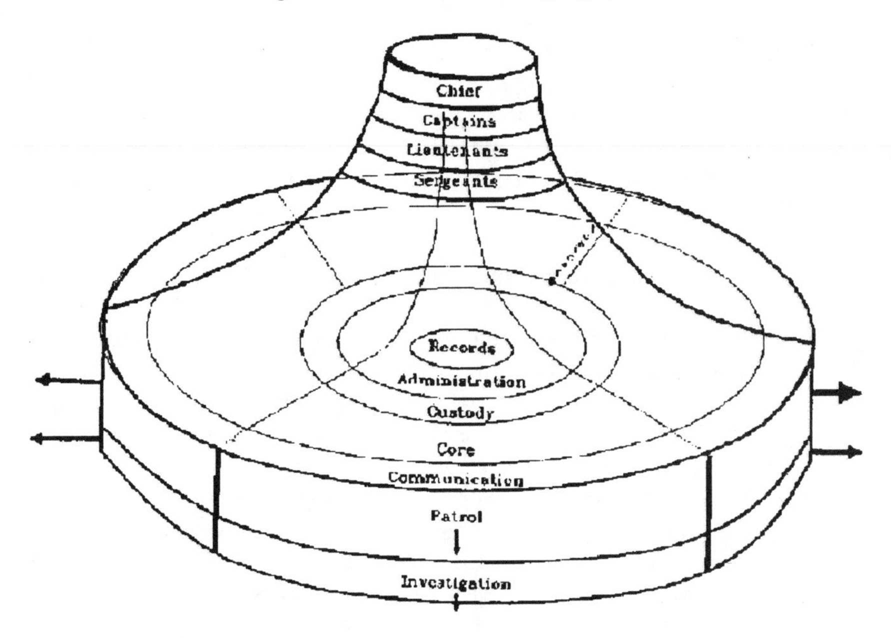

But hierarchy does matter here, too; the management at the centre is shown as flowing up, in order to "oversee" the operations, but necessarily with increasing detachment. Hence, while the culture may emanate from the apex, and may be protected and enhanced especially as it flows down the hierarchy, it comes to life at the outer perimeter, where the force meets the society.

As noted repeatedly, in the RCMP at least, this is about normative control. So let me close this description by contrasting this model of managing government with four others, some of greater historical significance, others more popular today, but all current.[21] The point I wish to make here is that it may well be time to welcome a return to more normative forms of control in government.

The Government-as-Machine Model

Government here is viewed as a machine dominated by rules, regulations and standards of all kinds, for purposes of legitimization, equality and conformity. This applies to the superstructure, the central state apparatus, for policy-making, budgeting, staffing, etc., no less than to the microstructures of each department or agency. The superstructure controls the agencies as the agencies control the activities. Government thus takes on the form of a hologram: examine any one piece and it looks just like the rest.

The machine model has been the dominant one in government, almost to the exclusion of everything else. As Frederick Taylor's "one best way," it was popularized in the 1930s in the public sector by Luther Gulick and Lyndall F. Urwick. Its motto might be "control, control, control."[22] In fact, the term bureaucrat, for civil servant, comes from the influence of this model.

The Government-as-Network Model

This is the opposite of the machine model: loose instead of tight; free-flowing instead of controlled; interactive instead of segmented. Government is viewed as one intertwined system, a complex network of temporary relationships fashioned to work out problems as they arise, linked by informal channels of communication. At the micro-structure level, work is organized around projects – for example, a project to develop a new policy on welfare or to plan for construction of a new building. "connect, communicate and collaborate" might be the motto of this model. Ironically, like the machine model, the network model is also holographic in that the parts function like the whole: individuals project function within a web of interrelated projects at the superstructural level.

The Performance-Control Model

Capital-letter "Management" finds its full realization in the performance-control model, the motto of which could be "isolate, assign and measure." This model aims above all to make government more like business. But we need to be specific here, because the business in mind implicitly is not just any business but rather the "divisionalized" structure, popularized by conglomerates. Here the overall organization is split into "businesses" that are assigned performance targets for which their managers are held accountable. Thus, the superstructure plans and controls, while the microstructures execute. All very tidy. But not necessarily very effective.

For one thing, few people in business today still believe in the conglomerate form of organizing. If the businesses have so little to do with one another, why bother to have them in the same organization? What value is added by a remote headquarters that exercises control of financial performance alone? For another thing, a heavy emphasis on planning and measured performance reinforces conventional hierarchical control at the level of the micro-structure, where managers are held personally responsible for attaining impersonal targets. The ultimate effect is to reinforce the old machine model.

In other words, the performance model decentralizes in order to centralize, loosens up in order to tighten up. And tightening up comes at the expense of flexibility, creativity and individual initiative. Thus the brave new world of public management all too often reduces to the same old world of machine management – new labels on the old bottles. And this works fine where machine management worked before, maybe even slightly better, for standardized, stable, simple, operating tasks, but nowhere else.

The Virtual-Government Model

Carry the performance model to its natural extreme and you end up with a model that can be called virtual government. Most popular in the United Kingdom, the United States, and New Zealand, virtual government assumes that the best government is no government. Shed it all, we are told, or at least all that is remotely possible to shed. In virtual government's perfect world, the microstructures would no longer exist within government. That would take place in the private sector. And the superstructure would exist to arrange for private organizations to provide public services. The motto of this model might therefore be "privatize, contract and negotiate."

The Normative-Control Model

None of the above models has succeeded in structuring social authority adequately. Perhaps that is because social authority is hardly about structure. So here is where the normative-control model comes in. It is not about systems but about soul. Attitudes count, not numbers. Control is normative – that is, rooted in values and beliefs.

This model is hardly front and centre in most Western governments these days, let alone in most Western businesses, which have retreated into the old machine model, or newer versions of it. And this is in direct contradiction to the normative model. Where there is still the concept of public service, however, this may well be the model that manages to keep governments functioning. For without service and dedication, no matter how tight the systems, how demanding the measures, government would come to a halt.

Five key elements appear to characterize the normative model:

Selection. People are chosen by values and attitudes rather than just by credentials.

Socialization. The membership is socialized to ensure dedication to an integrated social system.

Guidance. People are guided by accepted principles rather than by imposed plans, by visions rather than by targets.

Responsibility. All members share responsibility. They feel trusted and supported by leaders who practise a craft-style of managing that is rooted in experience. Inspiration, now so-called empowerment, thus becomes paramount.

Judgement. Performance is judged by experienced people, including recipients of the service, some of whom sit on representative overseeing boards.

The motto of the normative model might be "select, socialize and judge." But the key is dedication, which occurs in two directions: by and for the providers of the service. Providers are treated with decency and so respond in kind. This allows for radically different microstructures: more missionary, egalitarian and energized; less machinelike and hierarchical.

There is no one best model. We currently function with all of them. Tax collection would be inconceivable without a healthy dose of the machine model, as would foreign policy without the network model. And no government can function effectively without a significant overlay of normative controls, just as no government today can ignore the need to shed what no longer belongs in the public sector.

But some models are for the better and some for the worse right now. We all recognize the excessive attention given to the machine model. But we should be aware of its resurgence in the performance model. This is not to dismiss the performance model. The quasi-autonomous executive agency is fine for many of the apolitical, straightforward services of government – such as the Passport Office. Let's just keep it there and not pretend it is some kind of new "best way."

We need to be more appreciative of the network model, which is necessary for so many of the complex, unpredictable activities of today's governments – much of policy-making, high-technology services, and research, for example. But reliance on this model can also be overdone. In France, both public and private sectors have long been dominated by a powerful and interconnected élite that moves around with a freedom and influence that is proving increasingly stifling to the nation. The network system in France could use a lot more agency autonomy to check the power of that élite.

It is my belief that we sorely need a major shift of emphasis to the normative model. There is simply no substitute for human dedication. And although much of Western business needs to take this message to heart, it has become especially important in government, with its vagaries, nuances and difficult trade-offs among conflicting interests. An organization without human commitment is like a person without a soul: skeleton, flesh and blood may be able to consume and to excrete, but there is no life force. Government desperately needs more life force – not an obsession with the normative model, but at least a chance to take its rightful place.

The message of these three days with managers of the RCMP is that, not only is the normative model alive and very well, at least in pockets of contemporary government, but that it is what many other parts of today's governments, and, in part, all of today's governments, should look like.

4

Managing Policy

This chapter takes us to a part of government that has to combine operations with a significant policy-making component. As we shall see, that renders management that much more complex. The federal Department of Justice "manages the law," including the carrying out of litigation on the part of the federal government. At the time of this observation, the department employed 2,250 people, including 1,000 lawyers, making it, in part, a kind of super-law partnership. Two to three hundred lawyers were in court every day. In its "organigram," one could find a clearly distinguished set of policy units – criminal law, policy, administrative law reform, native law, environmental issues, etc. – grouped into sectors such as public law and criminal and social policy, next to an extensive hierarchy in the litigation sector, comprising civil, criminal, and tax law branches, etc., as well as regional offices around the country.

Two managers of the department were observed: the deputy minister and the head of one of its policy sections.

JOHN TAIT, DEPUTY MINISTER OF JUSTICE AND DEPUTY ATTORNEY GENERAL OF CANADA, OTTAWA, 18 MARCH 1993

"I find management very hard; I'm probably not a natural manager," John Tait told me first thing in the morning. He talked of taking a Myers – Briggs test with a number of other government managers, where he came out on the feeling side of one scale, while everyone else, including one woman, was on the thinking side. Upward feedback showed him as hesitant to come down hard on weak performers, he added.

John, who is a lawyer, came from the policy-adviser side, not the operations side. He was with the Privy Council Office before moving to Justice ten years ago and into his job as deputy minister four-and-a-half years ago. In fact, he returned to the Privy Council not long after.

This was an unusual day because of my presence. Whether by design or simply taking advantage of free time in his schedule, John devoted a great deal of time to discussion with me. As a researcher, I should perhaps have discouraged this. But that was his preference and it offered the opportunity to pursue the research agenda by interview as well as by observation, even if there was some contamination of the latter.

John had been terribly ill a short time before – he had gone into hospital on a relatively minor matter, but the day before he was due to be discharged his condition suddenly went out of control and over time became extremely serious. He stayed there seven weeks and had only come back to work two months previously. So he was in a reflective mood, and perhaps my presence offered him an opportunity to think about his work in a different way. He used to work an eighty-hour week, he said, but since the illness, was trying to hold it to fifty-five hours maximum, including a maximum of five hours on the weekends.

At 8:45 a.m. – we had both arrived at 7:50 a.m. and had chatted since then – his own immediate team came in, including his administrative and executive assistants. Most of the conversation took place between John and his executive assistant, with John going over various issues concerning people and scheduling until she raised her own issues, while the others listened. Then they did a quick go-around, and the meeting ended at 8:55 a.m.

We chatted some more, about the nature of the department and its need for teamwork, not only on the policy side but in litigation as well, as law was becoming more and more specialized. As John put it, with regard to the need to operate in an integrated way in the face of growth, "The territorial imperative is killing us."

At 9:20 a.m., his secretary brought in a courier package, and John got on the telephone, discussing a particular case in court and providing advice (e.g., "You're right in pulling out all the stops."), as well as offering help ("O.K. – I'll get a meeting of my key people on the litigation."). This was an official of another department who was being attacked in court by a private interest-group and who needed "a little hand holding."

At 9:40 a.m., Mary Dawson, who headed up the Public Law Sector, came in with her executive assistant, and they were joined by one of John's assistants. This was one of the regular meetings that John tried to hold with his sector heads, about once every three weeks, to review issues, discuss programs, and convey his own wishes and priorities. Here, as throughout the day, the discussion was very much issue-oriented, but sometimes these issues were of a very conceptual nature.

The meeting began with a discussion of "individual versus collective rights," an important issue with regard to current concerns of native peoples, among others. "People are all over the map on this, and I think the judges are too." Mary was supervising a paper on it, and John was providing guidance as to what he wanted. She came with a draft report on which he had commented extensively, and he was clarifying some of these comments for her. Then they moved on to "Crown liability," and the discussion shifted somewhat to management, with Mary advocating procedure and discussing people and John prodding her on some aspects while she was trying to gain clarification of what he wanted. Other issues continued in the same vein – self government, judges' salaries, priorities, etc., the latter offering a chance for Mary to talk about her job and John to express his expectations. With the comment "That was heavy going, I'll see what I can do," Mary left at 11:05 a.m.

There followed a meeting with Richard Mosley, who headed up the Criminal Law and Social Policy Sector, while John's executive assistant took the notes this time. This was a chattier, more relaxed exchange, some sharing of information before they again settled down to the specific agenda (e.g., firearms negotiations, native gaming), beginning with Richard's request that John clarify some written comments he had made on a draft paper. John seemed to be reviewing progress and getting himself informed while conveying his wishes, whether about a specific issue (e.g., "The reason I'm pushing you on this – just to tell you what's in the back of my mind – is ..." followed by comments on the background context of an issue) or about administrative process (e.g., "I think deadlines concentrate the mind wonderfully, and I like to see the mind concentrated.").

This meeting ended at 12:15 p.m., and, after "dealing with a couple of urgent things here," related to calls about a cartoon in a newspaper that some people had found offensive, with the decision made not to do anything but to be prepared for questions in Parliament that afternoon, and a bit more discussion between us, we headed to John's car at 12:40 p.m., to be driven to an Ottawa restaurant.

There John was to have lunch with Tim Plumptre, who was seeking the support of John and his department for Tim's non-profit Institute on Governance. I have known Tim for some years, and part way through the lunch, after the comment of "With your $10,000 John, we'd do even better," he turned to me and said "This is the hit, Henry!" John promised to check his year-end budget for the money and Tim gave him a form he could sign. Otherwise the discussion ranged across various specific and general issues of government.

We returned to the office at 2:30 p.m., where John met two of his people about a dispute with a provincial law society about credentials. Again

John provided guidance: "I think we should go step-by-step and not bring out our nuclear bombs." They discussed a letter that had been drafted for his signature, the contents of which he had toned down.

These people left after a few minutes, and at 3:05 p.m. we headed out the side door to the Supreme Court building next door. There the unveiling of a portrait painted of the recently retired head of the Federal Court of Canada was to take place. He had, in fact, been John's immediate predecessor as deputy minister of justice. A cocktail party was held after the ceremony, and John went around networking, discussing legislative changes with the chief judge of the tax court and chatting about a lecture series at Cambridge University. Then he headed back to his office, at 4:10 p.m.

From 6:30 p.m. to 10 p.m. that evening, John had a meeting to discuss briefing materials concerning the election that had to be called soon. The rest of the time we spent in discussion, particularly about parts of the job I did not see that day. John met approximately weekly with the minister, he said, for purposes of advising; had two or three meetings a week on average with other ministers or deputy ministers; and every two to three weeks went to the operations committee of cabinet, which met every Monday morning. He chaired a key meeting of federal and provincial deputy ministers of justice as well.

John said he tried to restrict his access to individual outsiders, preferring that one of his deputies saw them, although he did see academics, judges and people from the Canadian Bar Association occasionally. He also said he spoke formally twice a year to the Canadian Bar meetings, as well as to other national organizations such as the Federation of Law Societies, and tried to meet with the chief justice of the provinces and the deans of law schools periodically. He also made sure to speak to classes attending his own department's lawyer- and manager-training programs.

He said "We are still going through a culture change in this organization – I feel my job is to lead it," especially considering the more conservative nature of some of his people.

As for the mail, he said he received about eighteen inches per day and fifty inches per weekend, excluding legal periodical indexes and books. In Justice, "everything is in writing!" He had to see everything the minister was to see, including all positions the department took on, Supreme Court cases and all documents going to cabinet, not to mention that he had to approve formally all the travel expenses of his deputies. Financial documents alone he figured amount to several inches weekly.

Shifts in the justice system, especially interpretations by the courts that, in recent years, amounted to the making of policy, complicate his job, in John's view. Ministers wanted him to "do something," especially when the department's lawyers lost a key case. On that note, John headed for his meeting of senior officials.

Split Management

This was a very different job from the others so far described, much more involved with the intricacies of government, as opposed to the administration of it. John was a manager, to be sure, but as an expert on the law, he was also an important player in the political system of Ottawa, with regard to both policy analysis and the management of legislation. And that, I believe, influenced profoundly how he practised his management.

Deputy ministers in Ottawa have two rather different jobs to perform, which can require quite different styles. One is to manage the department as the most senior full-time employee, whether as a kind of de facto chief executive officer or else reporting to a minister, who seeks to play that role rather than a kind of chairman of the board. But either way, the deputy ministers are at least chief operating officers, responsible for the administration of the department and the implementation of its policies. And the other role is to serve as adviser to the minister on matters of policy as well as on briefing the minister for Question Period in Parliament – generally a very sensitive and time-consuming role. It may not be fair to ask the same person to do both jobs, but that has been the nature of the civil service in parliamentary democracy.

John's job was complicated by a third role. Because policy is so important here, and because the deputy minister of justice is often an expert policy analyst, as was John, that too became a key part of the job. Here the leader cannot just sit and delegate, and so John was seen to be a rather hands-on manager this day.

These three roles are illustrated in Figure 4.1 – advising up to the minister, administering down to the department, and analysing policy all around. These roles look different because they are different, which should raise fundamental questions about this job. Good policy analysts may not necessarily be good managers, and vice versa, while good advisers may be something else again.

We might step outside of Justice for a moment to ask if one of these roles – that of administering down – is actually necessary in many government departments. In other words, should departments be managed at all – as organizational activities?

I have in mind here those departments that are fundamentally conglomerate, such as Transport, or Heritage, and many others. We know from all sorts of unhappy experiences in business that conglomerates are mostly unmanageable, except by the sheer force of personality of the per-

Figure 4.1 *Split Management*

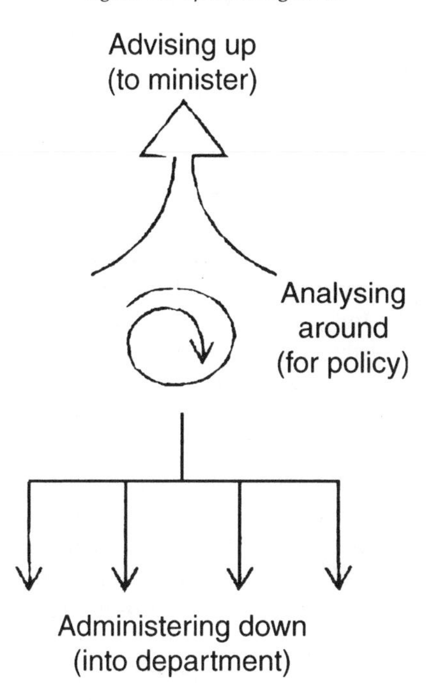

son who put them together. So why is so much government organized in this way? Presumably to keep the size of the cabinet manageable, by having a limited number of departments. Activities must be combined together so that they can report to a single minister and, in turn, deputy minister. In Transport, for example, air transport is combined with sea transport, which is combined with ground transport. It all looks so perfectly logical on paper, just the thing that warms the hearts of policy analysts in Treasury Board and the Privy Council Office. But what have air, sea, and road transport to do with each other, anymore than any one of them has to do with environmental issues or, for that matter, heritage, whatever that is?

Now, this would not be a problem if it is recognized this for what it is – a game of shuffling for convenience. Trouble is, people often do not. We live in an age of "Management" (with a capital letter), in which Managers are expected to Manage, even if the entity is unmanageable. So, deputy ministers run around calling meetings of people on air, sea and ground transport to develop common "plans," or to find "synergies."

Recall the discussion of "unnatural" managerial units in the last chapter. Most government departments are unnatural in this regard. The people who manage the natural units, such as air transport in the Transport Department, or parks in the Heritage Department, would appear to be better left free to manage as they must. They are the ones who should be the chief executive officers, and the deputy ministers should act like board chairmen, appointing effective managers and leaving them rather free to manage.

People become deputy ministers because they are energetic, and an energetic person with little to do can be a dangerous person, running around looking for those synergies. Recall the comment in Chapter 2 in Parks about "writing down the word heritage everywhere [they] could" in documents headed for Ottawa. When Parks reported to Environment, that had to get their attention. Then it was Heritage. But why must the Parks be pulled to Environment or to Heritage or to Industry or to Native Affairs any more than, say, to Tourism? If such agencies were overseen by boards of directors made up of the deputy ministers of all the affected departments, then perhaps these silly games could stop. The implication is that deputy ministers of conglomerate departments would do better acting as advisers to the minister than as managers of the department.

Justice is a focused and not a conglomerate department, so these roles, especially that of policy analyst, apply differently. And so John felt the pressures, especially being in Justice, this highly delicate domain in today's society. Perhaps there is the need for a kind of team management, where two or three people could share the deputy minister's job by working very closely together, literally in the same office.

Let us now take a look at the roles of this job as they appeared in this study.

Partly because of the key needs for policy analysis and advising and partly because of the incumbent's own background and predispositions, there was a stronger emphasis on conceiving and controlling in this job. John's background in policy analysis and his own training as a lawyer, not to mention the fact that he headed an organization of lawyers, naturally brought the conceiving part of the job to the fore. But this conceiving seemed, on this one day at least, more focused on specific issues than on general strategy. The frame of the job might thus be described as clear with regard to these individual issues and very much determined by the incumbent himself, in accordance with the wishes of the government and his minister, to be sure.

In a sense, ironically in terms of our model of managerial work, the conceiving connected closely to the doing, for what the Justice Department does, among other things, is to conceive, namely policy positions. In a sense, much of what any government does is to conceive policy positions and then turn them into legislation. In other words, here, doing is thinking, and thinkers, therefore, become doers! And because John seemed to play a rather hands-on role in this, some of his conceiving seemed to get close to doing.

All managerial jobs focus on issues, as described in Chapter 1 in the scheduling role of the model. But none I have seen to date puts specific issues into such a prominent position. Again, this is the nature of policy analysis. But it may also have to do with the practice of law itself, which is not only among the most analytical of professions, certainly the most verbal, but also one predisposed to decomposing its work into specific "cases," which, in common law, determine policy through precedent. Of course, the same is true of legislation itself, which requires extensive decomposition, not to mention articulation, in the most analytical of ways. But, then again, it is lawyers who write most of the legislation. With reference to research on the two hemispheres of the human brain, with verbal processes and so, presumably, analytic thinking concentrated on the side of the brain that controls the right side of the body, it may not be a coincidence that the French word for law, *droit*, is also the word for right. So a number of factors converged here to encourage decomposition and a rather analytical style of managing.

This, I believe, had an effect on the interplay of leading and controlling, for what I saw was technically closer to the latter than to the former. There was not as much effect or emotion in John's exchanges with his people as I saw in the work of most of the other managers I observed. But there was more of what I would call informing and advising here. And these came closer to the controlling role, which includes developing systems, designing structures, and making choices, as well as issuing directives. The last seemed especially important here: promoting certain directions in the decisions of others, especially by delegating specific duties and authorizing specific proposals. John's managerial style seemed to be one of conveying his specific wishes and beliefs and sometimes issuing more specific directives (e.g., "So I'd like you to consider that and if you could get back to me with a note ..."). He appeared to push his preferred positions along, issue by issue, in a manner that might be described as deductive.

The role of leading, pushed to the limit, is all effect and no content. Controlling, pushed to the limit, would be the opposite. John was not at the other extreme, but closer to it than to pure leading – much content with some effect. Of course, as one gets closer to the specifics, controlling becomes doing, as when John toned down the letter to the provincial law society, so that, as noted earlier, there was a doing element to John's involvement with issues as well.

Linking and dealing were a part of this job too. Networking was important, and there were apparently numerous contacts especially with policy-makers in government – perhaps more as a systematic constituency than as a loose agglomeration of contacts. But again, much of this seemed to concern specific issues too, so that, again, it connected the conceiving role of the job with its dealing role.

GLENN RIVARD, GENERAL COUNSEL, FAMILY AND YOUTH LAW POLICY SECTION, DEPARTMENT OF JUSTICE, OTTAWA, 23 SEPTEMBER 1993

Glenn Rivard ran the "Section" – thirteen people in all – concerned with policy about family and youth law in the department. He did this specialized work himself, although he was instrumental in creating the section in the first place when the work built up to justify it. Glenn reported to the chief, Policy Council for the Criminal and Social Policy "Sector," who in turn reported to the deputy minister.

This would seem to be a classic staff function – doing analysis and advising on policy – except that because this was part of the very mission of the Department of Justice ("Provide high-quality legal services and counsel to the government and to client departments and agencies"), among other statements, the unit here was clearly and centrally line. An official sheet of paper on "policy development" described "the normal steps whereby policy becomes law": a workplan is approved, research, analysis and consultation undertaken, and policy options developed; these are presented to the minister, who decides the preferred option and who seeks cabinet approval for it. Cabinet, in turn, decides policy and issues authority to draft the legislation, after which the bill is drafted by the Justice Legislation Branch and introduced to Parliament.

The day began at 8:30 a.m., at the Justice Building, just down the street from the building housing the Canadian Parliament in Ottawa. We chatted for awhile, Glenn commenting that policy analysis "is the point where the bureaucracy hits the political process." This was close to election time, which was quiet, he said. There was no Question Period in Parliament now: the politicians were focused more on party policy than government policy. Things tend to be hectic before this, he said, when there is a push for policy analysis and more emergencies occur to which the policy analysis people have to respond.

Glenn described this as a tricky business, so the rule is to try to funnel everything through the deputy minister, although issues of great interest, such as the Young Offenders Act, sometimes require dealing with the minister's office directly. At the outset of new legislation, the formalities of "policy development" notwithstanding, it is difficult to know what the

Figure 4.2 *The Legislation Field of Forces*

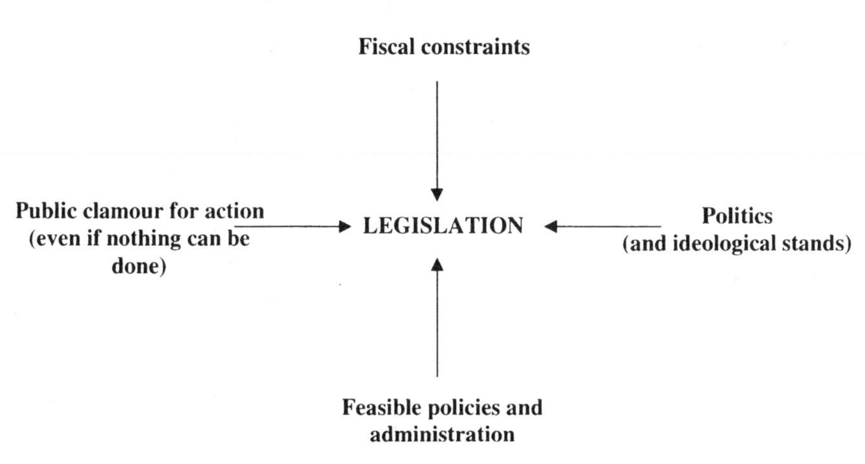

thinking is in the minister's office, since the people there tend to play their political cards close to the chest. "You really have to be literate on where this party – and other parties – stand on the issue," as well, of course, as where the Canadian public stands. So there is the need to read press clippings every day. "You're guessing – where does the government come from on this – and you're sending up options." In effect, the legislative situation sits in a field of forces, as shown in Figure 4.2.

This stands in contrast with Parks Canada in Chapter 2, whose people managed "on the edges," in the centre of political pressures. Justice is "somewhat removed from the fray," Glenn said, although "the issues you deal with are just as intense." Trade-offs have to be made even if positions can be rather "absolutist." But these are more distant from the operations, and the issues tend to be more abstract. Hence, according to Glenn, the consultation process can be used to try to broaden competing points of view to achieve some kind of consensus. This is characteristic of Canadian politics in general, and Glenn said that it is the role of the independent analysis prepared by his unit. "Often you see your role as looking past the interest groups to see broader consensual feeling." He did also note that positions on some issues seem to have become more ideological and political in recent years.

In a sense, while Parks often has to confront a choice, Justice can develop a policy. This may offer more latitude, at least for those adept at manœuvring through opposing positions. So in this job, while they used to be able to operate more in isolation, with less consultation, now Glenn felt that "a great deal of effort" had to be invested "to make linkages."

Glenn managed a portfolio of policy studies around "children files": child support, custody, child abuse, trafficking in children, marriage and family relations, even new reproductive techniques, which required a medical/legal expert on his staff. These involved policy analysis, concerning new legislation especially, but more and more he found people coming for advice, even beyond strict legal policy. Children's issues were coming to be viewed more broadly, in terms of their impact on society and also in terms of the number of agencies dealing with them, including ones of the United Nations with which Glenn also had to work.

Forty minutes had passed, and the phone rang at 9:10 a.m. The call concerned a WordPerfect demonstration; Glenn decided that he and his secretary would attend, and he scheduled a time. Then he turned to his voice mail, taking a message about an internal presentation. After that he called an officer of the Children's Bureau in the Department of Health to discuss a corporal punishment issue that suddenly surfaced. They discussed an upcoming meeting that she was to attend and the need to keep the discussion focused (for example, they didn't want to get into "spanking"!) and to coordinate their positions vis-à-vis the external contact groups that would attend, as well as with the media. The issue could obviously be delicate, especially with the election looming, and they were trying to pre-empt a blow-up.

Glenn was off the phone by 9:30 a.m., and Lisa Hitch, one of his legal counsel, dropped in momentarily on a scheduling issue, while another legal counsel called about consensus reached in a new steering committee. Glenn gave his view on how to rewrite a document and said he preferred to avoid chairing the committee. A few minutes later, Lisa came back in, and they discussed a variety of things, including various people and how they were reacting to situations, with her giving Glenn her opinion. On a paper someone was doing, Glenn said "I'm feeling intensely uncomfortable about the passage of time." Lisa said, "He's not rushed," and Glenn asked "Where did you get that impression?" expressing some concerns about the upcoming election.

At 9:45 a.m., Bernie Starkman, the section's medical legal specialist (half-time), appeared for his biweekly meeting, and Lisa left soon after, having dealt with a few common scheduling problems. Glenn and Bernie reviewed the Rodriguez case. Sue Rodriguez was a woman in British Columbia dying of Lou Gherig's disease, who had very publicly challenged the government in the courts on her right to euthanasia. In these discussions, Glenn seemed very attuned to the political dimension and was fairly directive, making a variety of requests.

At 10:03 a.m., Marilyn Bougard, in charge of the custody and access project in the section, came in, "briefly," because they spoke yesterday, and she told him about a meeting of the Advisory Council on the Status of Women and a United Nations report on NGOs concerning children. Like the others legal counsels, she seemed knowledgeable, informal and confident, briefing Glenn while he asked some questions as well as gave advice in response to some of her questions, which at times became more directive. ("I think it should be put in there." or "Maybe you should talk to Lisa on that.") She left at 10:24 a.m. – having been less "brief" than the others! – but Glenn called her back because he forgot to give her a "package of stuff the solicitor general is working on."

Then Glenn reached Aaron Caplan on the telephone, head of the Statistics Section in Justice. They chatted for about ten minutes on a variety of issues, including some statistical material for a book being done on Young Offenders. From the discussion, it was obvious that they worked closely together. There were a couple of other calls, one to convey a message from Aaron's call about the document that was coming, and then, at 10:43 a.m., Brian and Hillary, who dealt with family violence and child sexual abuse, respectively, in the section, came in. Glenn asked them to look over a document concerning a repealing of the prohibition on anal intercourse, went over a set of reports to check which they had seen, and informed them on the call to the person at the Department of Health. Then it was Hillary McCormack's turn; she had many items on her list: briefing Glenn on a meeting with police chiefs and judges out west; informing him of a talk show she was doing at noon on "what legislation can and cannot do"; and on a person visiting from Scotland ("Would you like to meet him?" at 2 p.m.); asking him if he had succeeded in getting the Treasury Board to reallocate some money to another account (no progress yet); debating with him on issues of prohibition versus pardon concerning change in a piece of legislation; and, finally, discussing who would take over her work after she left. The meeting ended at 11:48 a.m., a little over an hour in all.

"I just have to get through these few things," Glenn said as he signed a briefing note for the minister and went through the daily departmental press clippings. Then someone came in at 11:55 a.m. for a minute to introduce a friend visiting from Slovenia, part of a program with the Canadian Bar Association to bring in East European lawyers so that they can get a sense of the legal systems in the West. After an attempted call and a couple of voice messages, we left for lunch at 12:10 p.m., where the two of us talked about Glenn's job. "I can give people a lot more freedom if I know what's happening," Glenn said in response to my description of a "craft"-style of managing. Some people, he said, inform naturally, while others don't, so you need to see them regularly. Glenn read proposals to ensure they didn't "go off the rails" and to factor in the broader perspective that he had in his job, although he did claim to monitor some of the more important files closely, such as that concerning young offenders, where he was concerned about the approach that had been taken.

Asked about other work he did, Glenn discussed answering questions for other departments, or other units in his own department, as well as the minister's office, but less regularly. He said he did not see lobbyists much, who tended to "go above," to the minister, or "below," to the person working on the issue itself. He was involved with the Canadian Bar Association, which examines law reform and comments on it, and sat on various interdepartmental committees, including ones on family violence, child support, and marital and family issues, that he chaired, as well as on a departmental group on new reproductive techniques, which he also chaired.

We returned at 1:35 p.m., and after Glenn took a personal call, we looked over his agenda of a few months back. On 1 April, he had an all-day meeting on juvenile prostitution, with a federal and provincial umbrella criminal law group, and, on 2 April, the agenda showed an afternoon meeting to wrap up an earlier conference, "Legal Trends," which Glenn had chaired.

The following week had begun with a morning staff management meeting, followed by an afternoon ad hoc working group concerned with legislation about stalking. The minister had made this issue a priority and wanted something done before the election, so they had to introduce legislation quickly. Thus, all day that Tuesday they had met with women's groups. Wednesday's agenda had showed a section meeting, which happened every two weeks (the sector met weekly), a meeting with provincial representatives on the stalking legislation, and another on tax and child support guidelines. Thursday had had a section meeting, plus lunch, with Glenn's boss and a fellow from the minister's office about the Young Offenders legislation. There had been nothing scheduled for the Friday.

Things had continued more or less like this for the following two weeks: meetings with Hillary and Brian, other meetings on the stalking issue and on Young Offenders, the sector meeting and one of a working group on family violence. He had also met the minister to brief him on the child sexual abuse legislation, and the next day he had gone to a briefing by the minister to a parliamentary committee. This had been followed by a sector team-building lunch. There had also been meetings for the annual evaluations of his people, that part of his job he "hates the most" – he found the process artificial, preferring to meet with and review his people informally, which he said he did. Other activities had included "networking" with someone from administration of the department, a meeting with women from native groups about the Young Offenders Act, briefing the minister on the stalking bill and attending a press conference on it, he was there to listen and then to buttonhole key journalists to hand out and explain the document, a conference on legal trends, a meeting with provincial counterparts in Toronto on a variety of issues, a meeting of representatives from eight federal departments on the Young Offenders Act and another with a dozen members of Parliament to explain it, and a financial management course, part of the required training program for managers, "So I took that one." Glenn commented that "when the minister is here and things are humming a little faster, more people will drop in and there are more phone calls."

During this review of the April agenda, Hillary dropped in with the justice man from Scotland, concerned with child law there. He was particularly interested in the Young Offenders and sexual abuse legislation, and they shared their knowledge of practice and compared procedures in the two countries. That meeting lasted seventeen minutes.

By this time it was 3:15 p.m., and Glenn went to work on some yellow folders – another of his least favoured jobs: questions that came down from the minister's office that could not be answered, so his section had to do so. A number of telephone calls followed, about scheduling and one to approve a staffer's trip to Toronto, and then Glenn turned to the mail: an approval he had to sign, a paper entitled "Rounding Out the Manager's Job" that an academic had sent him, the record of a deputy ministers' meeting, law reports, a request to do a presentation and another to attend a conference in Australia – just a "mixed bag ... nothing really profound in it."

Glenn said that "when you are a specialist, you get a narrow range of documents and you read them all," but, now, "one of the most important tasks is knowing what not to read." At first, he tried to manage strategically, dealing with the broader, more abstract issues. But that didn't work, so now he found himself more involved. He orchestrated some of the bills himself, and, in other cases, chose the people to take the lead in their department, although there was very much of a "teamwork approach" – "we're all in it," he said.

At 4:05 p.m., Glenn had to leave to go to his son's school.

Conceptual Project Management

Glenn's was very much a job of project management in a rather delicate area of government legislation. Yet, the fact that the projects concerned policy instead of specific applications took a good deal of the heat off – at least compared to that experienced by the Parks people – so that, this day at least, I did not get a sense of intense pressure. Also, Parliament was not sitting. Conflicting interests certainly had to be reconciled in the work of this unit, but, as suggested earlier, there was more of the possibility to find creative solutions that integrated them.

Glenn managed lawyers and other professionals, who did part of their work individually – writing reports, drafting legislation, etc. – but who also had to work in teams. And so the structure of his unit, and indeed of the whole policy side of the department, seemed to look much like an adhocracy: project management in teams, producing customized outputs.[23] As Glenn noted, near the end of the day, that made his job of managing not so much detached and abstract as involved in the project work itself – overseeing it, reviewing it, and pushing it along, sometimes also doing it. In a sense, Glenn's unit had many balls in the air at any one time, and Glenn had to ensure that none fell down and that each sustained energy and eventually ended up where it should. Put differently, he managed a portfolio of projects and had to ensure that the projects are kept progressing.

On one side, then, the inside, there seemed to be a considerable amount of what Andy Grove of Intel has called "nudging," somewhat like leading, controlling and doing and, on the other, outside, the work involved a good deal of linking and communicating, including networking, briefing, informing, being informed and getting advice, etc.[24] This outside work was directed both to other government departments and to the minister's office, as well as to the rest of the Department of Justice, and to various interest groups and experts in the society at large. And then the inside and outside came together as Glenn factored the political and other dimensions (time pressures, links to other legislation, the broader perspective, etc.) into the work done in his section.

I also observed the head of a small film company in London. She too sat between the projects done by her people and the external situation whose dimensions she factored into that work. But, interestingly, she seemed rather hands-on externally and much less hands-on internally, perhaps because film-making involves tightly integrated project-teams handling rather less politically sensitive material, also because she had greater control over the selection of the people and the projects than did Glenn. She "did the deals" outside, whereas for Glenn there seemed to be no deals as such, or at least they were perhaps mostly "done" in the political process. And so it was linking per se that concerned Glenn.

As Glenn noted, he invested "a great deal of effort to make linkages." Someone had to keep track of all the external forces that had to be considered for legislation, and that was Glenn's job. He practised first-line project management, but, because of the nature of the work in question, this took place at a rather elevated level of analysis and abstraction.

Of the "boss," "professional," and "craft"-styles of managing, Glenn's style could hardly be called boss or professional, in the sense of detached "professional management." His work seemed clearly closest to craft, since he was involved and informed yet dealt with competent experts who knew what they had to do and did it, albeit with what sometimes seemed like close guidance from Glenn, especially if he had reason to be concerned about their experience or orientation to a particular project. But unlike the craft-style of the hospital unit head nurse whom I observed, here it was practised in a more conventional setting – this day, at least, in the confines of an office, often one-on-one or one-on-two, or else in a defined group meeting. All of this was, after all, about the practice of law, and just a few hundred metres from that most formalized of meeting places, the Parliament of Canada. Glenn commented in a letter in response to this analysis: "Your characterization of my managerial style as 'craft' would conform with my own view although, with pretensions I suppose, I have always thought of it as an 'art.' 'Craft,' however, is the better term, for it connotes a degree of functionality which 'art' does not. I think to some large extent this may be the product of the fact that I am managing the law and legal professionals. One cannot simply be a manager. One must also be a lawyer. And in the blending of the two, perhaps one gets 'crafty,' pun intended" (29 November 1994).

Reviewing the roles, communicating clearly stood out as key, as did linking. This was expert work, requiring a great deal of detailed knowledge about all kinds of things, especially external to the unit: the law in general, a host of specialized areas of the law pertaining to children and family, current conditions and sentiments in society in all of these areas, the wishes, moods, and inclinations of the politicians in power, associated activities in other government departments, and, indeed, other governments, in the provinces and around the world, and so on. Of course, linking also involved the outward flow of information as well as influence, for Glenn had to keep all kinds of external people informed about the activities of his unit, both to prepare them for its solutions and to promote those solutions.

Consistent with the craft-style of managing, the other roles here seemed often to blend together. Glenn clearly "did" the projects too, and there was no absence of controlling here, in the sense of issuing directives about his wishes on how certain projects were to be carried out, although control through systems was less in evidence – except, of course, through the systems imposed upon him by the Treasury Board and his own department. But mostly, this day at least, controlling, leading and doing seemed to blend somewhat together. This seemed to be in sharp contrast to the work of the deputy minister.

Project work is necessarily opportunistic, in that each project needs its own particular solution. This was clear in the work of the head of the film company I observed, and it seemed clear in Glenn's work too. That is not to say that a manager cannot impose his or her own predispositions on the work. Indeed, at one point Glenn showed me a report he did that called for more coordination and common understanding of family and youth problems in the department. So he managed a set of positions but with a sense of perspective.

The frame of this job can be described as adaptive, rather than fixed on one side or revolutionary on the other. That frame may seem to have been formally imposed; politicians are supposed to decide on the legislative agenda so that civil servants can develop it. But he seemed to have considerable room to manœuvre too. Bear in mind Glenn's comment about his role in the creation of the Family and Youth Law Policy Section in the first place.

Overall, the conceiving style can be described here as more inductive than deductive, as is the nature of law itself and especially making policy about it. However, the style was also rather cerebral, as the portfolio of projects unfolded over time to define, in emergent fashion, the strategy of family and youth law in Canada – guided, of course, by Glenn's own perspective.

Is Policy in fact Management?

We can conclude with a brief comment about policy versus management, for this was an issue especially here, although it seems to be endemic to government in general. That is why debates abound about whether senior civil servants should be analysts or managers and why the schools to train them are labelled both public administration and policy science. In business, in contrast, managerial skills are generally thought to be key, although the advent of so many MBAs, as well as the increasingly common trend of parachuting consultants into chief executive positions, is pushing business in somewhat the same direction, with perhaps similar problematic consequences.

Here we have two jobs in the same department of government, one at a more middle level, with more natural blending of the roles, the other at a senior level, more split between advising, analysing and administering. Part of this difference may have been due to the styles of the incumbents in question. But another part seemed to reflect the levels at which these jobs existed in the hierarchy, and this could be the cause of greater concern.

Historically, perhaps, policy mattered most. Today, perhaps, management matters more. But has this been properly reflected in appointments to senior positions in the civil service? And if – or when – it does, will that actually help matters? To end where we began, government is not business. Policy is critical, and good policy analysts as well as good policy advisers must be in senior positions in the civil service. But management is becoming more important as well as more complex. Government will have to develop its own approaches to management, or at least reinforce the effective approaches it has already developed. That means it must imitate business less, in structure at least as much as in style, in the arrangements by which managers work together, to analyse, advise and administer in coordinated fashion. I hope that the descriptions in these last three chapters will help point the way.

NOTES

1 Henry Mintzberg, "Rounding out the manager's job," *Sloan Management Review* 36, no. 1 (Fall 1994), pp. 11–26.
2 Henry Mintzberg, *The Nature of Managerial Work* (New York: Harper & Row, 1973). See also Henry Mintzberg, "Managerial Work: Forty Years Later," in S. Carlson, ed., *Executive Behavior* (Uppsala, Sweden: Textgruppen I, 1991).
3 Robert Simons, *Levers of Control: How Managers Use Innovative Control Systems to Drive Strategic Renewal* (Boston: Harvard Business School Press, 1995).
4 H.A. Simon, *The New Science of Management Decision* (Englewood Cliffs, N.J.: Prentice-Hall, 1960).
5 Luther Gulick and Lyndall F. Urwick, *Papers on the Science of Administration* (New York: Columbia University Press, 1937). See also Henri Fayol, *General and Industrial Administration* (London: Pitman, 1949). Translated from *Administration industrielle et générale*, published by Dunod, Paris, in 1916.
6 F.W. Roethlisberger and W.J. Dickson, *Management and the Worker* (Cambridge, Mass.: Harvard University Press, 1939).
7 M. Maeterlinck, *The Life of the Bee* (New York: Dodd, Mead and Company, 1918).
8 Leonard R. Sayles, *Managerial Behavior: Administration in Complex Organizations* (New York: McGraw-Hall, 1964); Mintzberg, *Nature of Managerial Work*; John P. Kotter, *The General Manager* (New York: Free Press, 1982).
9 Sayles, *Managerial Behavior*; Leonard Sayles, *The Working Leader* (New York: Free Press, 1993).
10 Tom J. Peters, *The Case for Experimentation or you can't plan your way to unplanning a formerly planned economy* [pamphlet] (Palo Alto, Calif.: Tom Peters Group, 1990); Michael E. Porter, *Competitive Strategy* (New York: The Free Press, 1980); Warren Bennis, *Leaders: The Strategies for Taking Charge* (New York: Harper & Row, 1985); Warren Bennis, *An Invented Life: Reflection on Leadership and Change* (Reading, Mass.: Addison-Wesley, 1993); Fayol, *General and Industrial Administration.*

11 Andrew Grove, *High Output Management* (New York: Random House, 1983).
12 Karl E. Weick, *The Social Psychology of Organizing* (Reading, Mass.: Addison-Wesley, 1979). See also Henry Mintzberg, "Crafting Strategy," *Harvard Business Review* 65, no. 4 (July/August 1987), pp. 66–75; Henry Mintzberg and J. Jorgensen, "Emergent strategy for public policy," CANADIAN PUBLIC ADMINISTRATION 30, no. 2 (Summer 1987), pp. 214–29.
13 This chapter has been previously published, under the same title but with modifications, in *International Journal of Public Sector Management* 10, no. 3 (1997), pp. 131–53. It is reprinted here with permission.
14 R. Raphael, *Edges: Backcountry Lives in America Today on the Borderlands between Old Ways and the New* (New York: Knopf, 1976), p. 16.
15 I was hiking a few days later with the owner of a rustic lodge in the back-country of a provincial park, a five-hour hike from the nearest road. As a helicopter whirred overhead, he commented on people who "have a nice lunch at the Banff Springs Hotel and then take a little tour of the Rockies in the afternoon." The edges can be thin indeed at these high altitudes!
16 In 1885, two years after some railway workers chanced upon some hot springs near what is now the town of Banff, the Government of Canada set aside an area around them as a park reserve.
17 Canada, Department of the Environment, Parks Canada, Western Region, "Defining our destiny: leadership through excellence" [draft document, 1993], pt. 2.1.
18 Henry Mintzberg, "Toward Healthier Hospitals." Working Paper, Faculty of Management, McGill University, 1995.
19 Linda Hill, *Becoming a Manager* (Boston: Harvard Business School Press, 1992).
20 M.L. Gimpl and S.R. Dakin, "Management and magic," *California Management Review* 24, no. 1 (Fall 1984), pp. 125–36.
21 Henry Mintzberg, "Managing government, governing management," *Harvard Business Review* 74, no. 3 (May/June 1996), pp. 75–83.
22 Frederick W. Taylor, *The Principles of Scientific Management* (New York: Harper, 1911); Gulick and Urwick, *Papers on the Science of Administration.*
23 Henry Mintzberg, *Structure in Fives: Designing Effective Organizations* (Englewood Cliff, N.J.: Prentice Hall, 1983), p. 2.
24 Grove, *High Output Management.*

PART TWO

Applying the Model: Observations and Discussion

5

Managing Publicly: Concrete Experiences[1]

Jacques Bourgault
Martine Éthier

Mintzberg's explanatory model of the public manager deserved to be tested empirically. We sent the Mintzberg texts to senior civil servants at all levels of government and asked them to participate in a roundtable discussion. They met in Montreal in late February 1998. Most of the participants had occupied several different high management positions in public organizations.

Present were Huguette Labelle, president of CIDA; John Tait, former deputy minister of justice; Ralph Heintzman, associate secretary of Treasury Board; Cécile Cléroux, executive director of the Centre Hospitalier de l'Université de Montréal; Pierre De Celles, executive director of ENAP; Diane Wilhelmy, associate general secretary of the Réforme administrative au gouvernement du Québec; Jean-François Léonard, vice-chair, UQAM; Jacques Duchesneau, chief of the CUM Police Services; Louis Bernard, vice-president of The Laurentian Bank; France Desjardins, president of the Régie du Logement; Nicole Fontaine, president of the Office du consommateur and president of the Public Administration Institute of Metropolitan Montreal; Mohamed Charih, study director, ÉNAP in Hull; Maurice Demers, director of research, Canadian Centre for Management Development; Daniel Maltais of the BFDR; Gérard Divay, executive director of the City of Montreal; and Joseph Galimberti, executive director of the Institute of Public Administration of Canada.

For purposes of clarity, the statements made by the participants were grouped according to the themes introduced in Mintzberg's model.

PUBLIC–PRIVATE: THE RIGHT STUFF FOR MANAGING PUBLICLY

The participants insisted on an analysis of the particular constraints placed on the public sector before examining its similarities and differences with the private sector. The assumption was that the environment of the public manager could have wide-ranging implications on management theory. The requirements of conformity, transparency and accountability were identified as particularly significant in understanding the public manager's role. The private sector's insistence on absolute results, while important in terms of public policy, can only be seen as one of many desirable outcomes in the world of public managers.

Louis Bernard: I would argue that the question raised by Mintzberg was fundamental at this time in Quebec society. I think his most important line is "management is management, managing is managing," and that it applies as much to the public sector as it does to the private sector. I have worked in both sectors, and I find the outline very useful in understanding what happens in both the public and the private sectors.

It is an important line, but it needs some nuance, so I would like to spend a minute to review the main concepts. I submit that the phrase is relevant to both the public and the private sectors. If we compare them, the distinction is that some duties in management are more important in the public sector while others are usually more important in the private sector. They are all present, I think, in both sectors. On the other hand, it would be quite difficult to pretend that "managing is managing" no matter where it takes place, because of the private sector's view of revenues. Clearly, they are not used to the same ends as in the public sector. If it were simply true that "managing is managing," we could apply the tools of success in the private sector and import them to the public sector. We cannot do this. In this sense, Mintzberg is right to add that "government is not a private enterprise." Government, overall, is the social life: while the private enterprise is a particular endeavour. Therefore, I think that while the first phrase is of limited use, we must also accept the second one.

More than thirty years ago, I was attending the London School of Economics, and William Robson was my professor. We had a post-graduate seminar and the theme was "is public administration unique?" For an entire semester we discussed what made public administration distinct and what made it similar to private management. A quick conclusion was that public managers, like private managers, cannot continually manage in public. No enterprise could make profits by managing everything in public; it is impossible.

Therefore, there must be a confidential zone in management. The same could be said about public management. The Ministers' Council, for example, cannot sit in public: it is, in fact, protected by constitutional principles that ensure a certain area of confidentiality. What is good for the Ministers' Council is, in many cases, good for a hospital, a "régie régionale," many public enterprises, for consumer protection, etc. We cannot think that because it is in the public sector, there is no area of confidentiality. I think management requires a certain area of confidentiality. This balance between what belongs to public administration and what belongs to any management must be found in our society at the present time. We must say: yes, this is unique, but, yes, this is also administration, because "management is management."

Let's look at Mintzberg's main concepts. When I look at the centre, "advising, analysing and controlling," I would say that in the public sector "advising" is more important; "analysing" is a little bit more important; "controlling" (in the sense of controlling the results) is more important in the private sector. Techniques for controlling results are more developed and more important in the private sector than in the public sector. Perhaps we should put more emphasis, in the public sector, on controlling measures and instruments. It would improve public administration.

We have put more emphasis on advising and analysing, less importance on controlling results. But if you want to improve things, you must improve the control. I would say that in the private sector, they should be more attentive to "analysing" and "advising," especially in their relationship with the outside world. They are not very good at it: the public sector is more prepared to do that. In terms of Mintzberg's "linking" and "leading," I would say that, in the public sector, the linking is more important, the leading is less important. In the private sector, it is the contrary: the leading is more important, the linking is less. About the "doing" and the "dealing," I would say that in the private sector, the doing is more important and, in the public sector, the dealing is very important because you are always dealing with somebody else, because of the complexity of the organization and because of the importance of the relationship with the outside world. When you put it all together, you have the same elements, but different proportions.

Henry Mintzberg: One day, Jacques Bourgault and I discussed the origins of the word management. We came to the conclusion that two sources had merged at a certain point. The original word came from the control of horses. In fact, the word "handling" comes from the word "hand" and *circa* 1600, designated the action of controlling horses. At that point, management as a concept became associated with control. During the seventeenth century, the French word *ménage* was confused with the word "manage" in English. Two meanings followed: *ménage* – to maintain a certain order in a place, I believe – and "manage." We often say in French that the language is flooded with English expressions, but often the reverse is true! (Take, for example, the word "budget": a *budget* in French was a purse worn on a belt; the word entered the English language and disappeared in French; it came back as budget in a financial sense.)

Ralph Heintzman: I much appreciated Louis Bernard's remarks, which prompted two more thoughts. First, he said he agreed with Mintzberg that "managing is managing, but the public sector is not the private sector, you can transfer the practice from one to the other." This reminded me that the report from the federal Deputy Ministers' Task Force on the Public Service Values and Ethics, chaired by John Tait, discussed the debate around the new public management. It concluded that there are two ways to look at a government or public service: it can be looked at from the top or from the bottom. If you look at it from the bottom, you have managerial concerns similar to those of the private sector. But if you are looking at it from the top, you are doing it from democracy, ministerial decisions, laws and rights, etc. An adequate view of the public sector must hold those two points of view at the same time. I think that this says exactly the same thing: "managing is managing" but "the public sector is not the private sector." There are those two "lenses," as we say, through which we can look at the public sector and we must have the two of them at the same time in order to be exhaustive in our perspective.

Diane Wilhelmy: Among the essential differences between public and private management, one seems more important to emphasize. Representatives of the private sector often remind us that the difference lies in the fact that in the public sector, we always manage in a glass house. In that sense, I think the performance expectations are becoming a little unrealistic. I would also add that when we think about the various public–private functions and roles, it is obvious that transmitting information has become an important part of public administration. Be it to a minister, a deputy minister, an executive director, to Parliament, the Office of the Auditor General, the Access to Information Commission, the ombudsman, the press, interest groups, or to the wider public, it is becoming very demanding and calls into question many public policies. It is very difficult for higher management to give, let alone retain, a clear and stable-enough vision. And yet that sort of consistency is necessary for first-line managers so that they can feel they are in control. They always feel that they have to conduct some sort of a review or audit "just in case," because this is not a system that is, say, clear enough to be translated simply down to the lowest level.

It is difficult to transmit this vision because in major public policy areas such as health, social services, education and welfare we have an incomplete consensus on what the scope of the reforms contains – particularly the reforms related to public finances. The role of a department or organization is then questioned by interest groups and the wider public, and it is very difficult to explain what it will mean in terms of services or procedures. Therefore, those who manage it daily are insecure.

INVENTING A JOB FRAME IN A DELIBERATIVE ASSEMBLY

The model begins with a person's values, experiences, knowledge and competencies and seeks to establish a particular job frame with its own purpose, interpretation of needs and strategy. Practitioners insisted on the vagueness and ever-fluctuating nature of the public manager's job frame, because it is dependent on political battles, public negotiations and a continual evolution of a public organization's mission. The fluidity of the public manager's job frame – particularly in light of fluctuating economic and social conditions – invited more reflection.

Cécile Cléroux: Nowadays, on the public side, we manage with a demand for public input that is hardly compatible with the scope of the current reforms. We have lost the sense of what the reality of democracy is, and we have bound our public managers not only to transparency but also to compromise. It has reached a point where our internal thinking processes are now totally twisted by an abusive exploitation of what the "influence on the course of decisions" means, in particular by the extensive use of media. Turbulent public council sessions such as those frequently held by the City of Montreal reveal how difficult consensus has become. With the implementation of reforms in the health system, hospital board sessions have been open to the public. I can tell you that it makes a great difference when there are reporters in the room – a situation that is analogous to talking to the most militant union officials instead of the employees who are actually affected by changes. Currently, we are dealing with a large-scale transformation in our hospital: we are merging three large institutions in a context of unprecedented budget cutbacks and creating a new university hospital [Centre hospitalier universitaire]. We really have no example to follow in Quebec, and this new concept must be adapted from American models. With a total inadequacy of means – we're trying to create American institutions without American resources – we are now doing all the policy work-up in full view of the public! Can you imagine the consequences?

Steering in the Storm

Gérard Divay: Diane Wilhelmy has already alluded to my central point, but I would like to develop it further. Let me borrow the imagery of a book that you know well, *Piloter dans la tempête*. I think that the major characteristic of public management right now is piloting in the fog, because there is a good part of indecision and confusion at all levels as to what should be the basic orientations. Trying to maintain cohesion among the troops and motivate people to work, despite the uncertain nature of the orientations, can be difficult. Moreover, we will undoubtedly be living with this situation for quite a long time. The thinking on the nature of the "core business" of the public sector has barely started. If we look in the different sectors, it seems that we can observe some consistency: more and more, the civil service is vacating the delivery aspect of public service even in the areas of education and health. We are going back to the classic mission of the state: not controlling people so much as controlling the environment in which free human beings can evolve.

A Job Frame through Management of Political Communities

Jean-François Léonard: Essentially, the university is a political site in the sense of the Greek city-state. The professors are the citizens and, of course, the organization functions according to a democracy of peers. The manager of this "university city," however, cannot control it in the traditional sense of the term. He can only reach limited consensus on particular operational and development objectives. Contrary to the Greek citizens of antiquity, the university citizens do not feel collectively responsible for the development of their city. They feel individually responsible for their career development and, in light of what is at stake for their career, will only act collectively to protect a nurturing environment. This being said, one of the significant evolutions in the environment of the public manager is the intense internal political pressure. This pressure comes from various sources, not the least of which is professors and students expecting support from the university. But pressure is also created by a confusion of understandings of the development objectives and of the operational process (scientists do not share the same vision of the university as artists or humanities professors – I get the feeling that they see themselves isolated as they face the challenge of proving their scientific credibility everyday).

Ultimately, it is in this context of widely differing approaches, interests and interpretations that the public manager's job frame is distinctly different.

Pierre De Celles: I would argue that, traditionally, public managers have focused on the internal dimension of administration. They also worked by using a deductive approach rather than an intuitive or inductive one.

Consequently, I found Mintzberg's idea of rebalanced weights and his analysis of the interaction between dimensions very interesting. I believe it would also be fruitful to show how the identified roles interact with each other and reinforce each other.

MANAGING THROUGH INFORMATION: ORGANIZATIONAL CAPACITY TO COMMUNICATE

Managing through information demands a formal process as well as a blend of informal managerial responses to the realities of the cultures of dissemination. Participants paid little attention to formal processes, except to emphasize their limits. Official messages imposed by political constraints are not credible in an environment that is consistently in flux. On some occasions, as some participants observed, management runs the risk of appearing outright hypocritical. Public managers must often practice a communication strategy of reconciliation with their employees.

The need for action may lead to a need to overcome organization charts, traditional lines of authority and formal job classifications. Public management is taking place in a context where the manager is held responsible for his actions, so he or she may take risks in choosing strategies and in choosing the right staff to execute decisions. Communication in this respect is vital: it gambles on overcoming accepted practices. It also challenges what is nothing less than a cultural understanding of work. Depending on how the process is managed and communicated, a manager may empower his best employees, or alienate them.

Nicole Fontaine: I would like to deal with the question of mission and vision. Over the last years, we have experienced a drastic transition: we have been managing in terms of objectives and important budget constraints. Politicians of every stripe have said: "We will cut, but we will maintain services." At the office, we responded accordingly: we kept first-line services, we "cut the fat," we cut the management! Our regional offices have remained in the field and have done the work in the most professional manner possible. The problem is that population needs are changing. By maintaining the first line and by cutting managers (who constituted the "fat"), we have cut the capacity for the organization to adapt and to adjust, because we let go a good part of those who were able to visualize what was happening, who were able to adapt, and who helped the organization adapt as a whole. Consequently, first-line services are still meeting the public's needs for the time being, but they are less and less adequate, because needs have changed. Moreover, the organization of the work has not been reviewed, because it is not up to the first-line workers to do it.

Leaders Stepping over Bureaucracy's Structures and Ladders

Diane Wilhelmy: Quebec managers who lived the 1998 ice storm in the most affected regions said the departments that performed the best were those that were the most regionalized: health, agriculture, transportation. These departments had already made strategic decisions and taken measures in light of their decisions. They were better prepared to react more rapidly to a new and extremely complex situation. During the Saguenay [River flood] crisis, I noticed another reality: Department lines were easily crossed in an emergency: the clients – the citizens – had to return home, and the roads had to be reopened for them. It is one of the realities of the public sector that in our immense bureaucracies we sometimes end up forgetting the client. In the private sector, by comparison, the client is always at the centre of the decisions. It seems that in public management, this capacity to "silo" the information, the mission and the *raison d'être* of what we are doing is even more obvious when we are suddenly part of a network with others who bring a new perspective. For example, in a retirement home, the food had to be inspected before it was given to the patients for fear of contamination. It followed, naturally, that the Agriculture Department had to be there, just like the Ministère de la sécurité publique (the equivalent of solicitor general's ministry in other governments), to inspect the food. Recently, I was told how conflicts between the inspection teams erupted and where natural managers succeeded in imposing their views by invoking the client's need. It would be interesting if these people would tell us how they overcame the rigidity of silo bureaucracy.

Informing: Being Directivist or Cultural?

Jacques Duchesneau: Commissioner Norman Inkster puzzled me a bit when he said in Mintzberg's text that he managed through the "no surprise" motto; it seems rather unfortunate because police organizations across America have been managed through the "no surprise" for too long. I would argue that this goal is deceiving because each morning when I wake up, I expect that the sky has fallen on my head! It is part of the police manager's job to expect that during the night one of his 5,700 employees has done something that could have grave consequences. In this sense, I see public managers sitting in an ejector seat but without the control button. There are 5,700 persons who can trigger the button, and it can be quite uncomfortable for a police force manager!

If we manage through the "no surprise" practice, there is a danger that our managers will become wet blankets. Inevitably, the culture will become one where people will say: "do not make noise, do not make waves, act so that my next promotion will not be questioned or refused. Do not ruin my career by doing something that could also have repercussions on us." The second potential consequence is that initiative will be lost. If police officers say, "The boss is paid to make decisions, then I will wait and when there is a major decision to be made, I will call somebody to make that decision." The example we all know is the tragedy at the École Polytechnique. There was a killer on the loose, and our first officers on scene were saying. "Let's secure the area and watch the situation. We will wait for the boss; he will tell us when to enter." I see this as a "no surprise" approach and such an attitude has major consequences. This situation has made Service de la police de la communauté urbaine de Montréal (SPCUM) proceed to major changes in the procedural norms and standards that diminished the sense of initiative that is essential to police work. The standards often pose an ethical problem, because there are too many rules, and the employees then think there is someone, somewhere who will seek solutions, thus relieving them about having to think in terms of solutions. We will never write all the guidelines necessary for every situation we encounter.

We must trust people. In the police, or in any other public organization, a manager must assume a part of the risk that is inherent to this function. If the person sitting in the ejector seat does not want to take the risks and chooses to manage through the "no surprise" approach, this person is not doing the job we expect of him or her. I choose orientations – a statement of the principles and values that we accept in the organization and that will guide the individuals, rather than plans that are imposed. We used to have plans decided by higher management and we had to find ways to implement them in the district, even if it could not be applied in the district. The global vision was stronger than the local goals. This has to change.

Judgement becomes all the more important. I would argue that performance is best assessed by experienced people rather than by procedures and guidelines. Four years ago, we had 926 procedures and guidelines. One procedure even indicated how to place the guideline manuals on the desk. Today, we have 75 procedures and guidelines, and we would like to decrease this number to one. In fact, the message that was sent to our people was confused. On one hand, we were telling them "We are giving you a gun, therefore you have the power to kill if need be and you have the power to take away freedom." At the same time, we told them "We will monitor you as if you have had no instruction and no judgement." Today, the job frames change daily because of decisions made by the various judicial, administrative and political authorities; our approach is to tell police officers to examine a situation under every angle possible in order to solve a problem.

Henry Mintzberg: Concerning central control, some say that there are a lot of reasons for life being easier in Prince Edward Island, because of its small size. This means that, in the end, it is not very expensive to manage a health system for 132,000 persons compared to that for a population of 6 or 7 million, essentially because it is less complex. What happens if, in order to manage its health system, Quebec would do exactly as the federal government does? What if Quebec said: we will have twenty-two people in Quebec City to manage the system overall, and then Laval will have a rather autonomous health system, which, just like PEI, manages itself. I choose Laval because it is an island: not as big as Montreal, but bigger in population than Prince Edward Island! We talk a lot about decentralization and the fact that the provinces need more powers. I think that a country with ten centralized governments is not a decentralized country. We have three levels of governments, and even if Quebec were to become independent, it would still have two levels of governments. How much power do the provinces devolve to the municipalities? Provinces have incredible control over municipalities. And we talk about decentralization!

MANAGING THROUGH PEOPLE

Leadership: Sharing Vision in the Midst of Turbulence

Participants observed that they had a supportive, rather than directive, leadership and that they mostly worked in a reactive, rather than proactive, context. The situation was exacerbated by the organizational instability created by the many changes brought to public services.

Huguette Labelle: It is very difficult for a senior manager to give a vision to employees if the organization is in constant mutation. It is really like a neurosurgeon: the president of the hospital will not come and tell him how to remove a brain tumour; the surgeon is expected to be able to do it on his own. We want the people who deliver public goods to be as professional as possible, in the purest, traditional definition, so that they require as little direction as possible. The role of the manager is to ensure that the objectives to be reached are clear and that the employees have the tools to realize it.

Jean-François Léonard: In an organizational and social context where there is a weakening or a lessening of the university professoriate's responsibilities vis-à-vis society, I cannot be, as Sandy Davis is in Mintzberg's text, an arbitrator in the university. I can only do my best to "activate people into action." I can only urge professors to develop their interactions with society in new, more creative ways. I only become the boss – in the traditional meaning of the term – when there is an ethical fault, when a deadline is not met, or when a research project is not evolving well. At that moment, as a manager, I take total control of the situation.

Managing Links with Environments

Pierre De Celles: I think that we cannot insist enough, in this world of links and interactions, on the particular role of the manager in making links with the environments. It essentially tries to apply the now-vanished boundaries (hierarchy, between internal and external, between various jurisdictions) to the new realities of public management. I think the situation could be more clearly explained if, in this world of links and interactions, the particular role of the manager could be emphasized and developed. Ultimately, it is probably this role that, among all roles, is likely to be most significant over the next years.

Gérard Divay: Cécile Cléroux argued that we are somewhat forced to manage in "an excess of democracy." I quite agree with her, and while I lived it at the provincial level, I have come to realize that it is even more obvious at the local level, where I work now. At the local level, each manager has his own networks and his own environment. That makes decision-making even more complex. Recently, I read an article on trends in the American media. The author noted that it is increasingly oriented towards local news. I think this is happening in Canada, and I would expect that in the near future, we will have to live with this aspect of "excess of democracy." My impression is that public pressure has a constantly growing role in the work of administrators. For managers today the question is to know how to offer a non-political treatment – since we have not been elected – to the kinds of pressures from organized groups, the press, the population, and even from elected officials. How can we ensure a non-political treatment of these political pressures? I would argue that, inevitably, the increasing importance of the public manager's linking role comes from the fact that our public and administrative institutions are obsolete compared to what must be done within the current socio-technological context. Should we not be asking if our institutions are still adequate? For example, it is definitely not obvious to me that education must be given through schools, and it is definitely not a given that a good health system must be delivered through a vast array of hospitals. There is some kind of explosion we must grapple with, as people's needs are more "holistic." But we have not yet found the formula to link the different specialized organizations with the "whole person" needs of specific clients. My impression is that we will see, mainly at the local level, interesting efforts in creating these links. Unfortunately, very sectorial institutions remain strong. The time for a reorganization of the public sector is coming.

Jean-François Léonard: I think the theme of cultural reorganization needs to be raised, and I can relate to this in the context of my work at the university. It never ceases to amaze me how the universities in this country are deeply rooted in the middle ages. My main role is to create a link, an interaction between the internal and external environments. These environments have needs and requirements in terms of training and research that follow the rhythm of the development of knowledge economy: they must be immediate and imperative. This pulsating rhythm crashes against the internal culture of the university, which wants to be democratic, involved, characterized only by its intellectual dynamics. The university manager must therefore reconcile this internal culture with external culture and needs. This creates a tension all the more intense because without the cooperation of the professors, the manager can do nothing; he cannot obtain a contract or create a strategic alliance. Contrary to Sandy Davis's management style, the shock of these two cultures forces university management to be essentially "opportunist." Ultimately, rules and policies barely have a hold over university professors.

Jacques Duchesneau: The Montreal police reports to a public-security commission. It is deeply aware of the issues, and, in turn, it reports directly to the municipal governments. The island has twenty-nine municipalities, which means twenty-nine city councils and twenty-nine back-seat drivers who scrutinize us closely.

It is interesting to compare this situation with the RCMP's organizational chart, which has many authority levels. It looks as if it is managed by officers who have been there for twenty-five, thirty or thirty-five years. It is an organization where, in the end, elected representatives have little input on internal management. Paradoxically, at the SPCUM [Service de la police de la communauté urbaine de Montréal], it is somewhat the contrary. Our authority levels have been decreased from nine to only four, and all the operational authority is actually given to the police officers in each of the forty-nine districts in the territory. However, elected representatives have a lot to say about our operations, namely through the public-security commission.

How can we explain that? Basically, the police force has two functions: investigation and patrol work. It is worth noting that the RCMP is decentralized in the sense that it very often acts as a municipal and provincial police force and that in its decentralized activities it has faced very few political consequences. In the area of investigation, on the other hand, it deals with national and international investigations, which have more repercussions at the political level.

For a municipal force such as ours in Montreal, it is the contrary. For police activities, we have more input from elected representatives because they are called directly by the citizens about any disturbance (speeding, noise, etc.). Thus, this explains why the RCMP is decentralized at the police work level, but that at the investigation level, it remains highly centralized, because each activity could have national political consequences.

John Tait: I really liked the standardized model explained by Henry Mintzberg. I think that it is a good model that can explain many public-sector organizations. However, the more we work with ministers, in departments, for example, the more difficult it is to implement the model, because ministers do not want headlines in newspapers saying that something was badly managed or that we have spent too much or that we did not treat a citizen with respect. Our employees know that; they are intelligent and they are nervous. They find us very hypocritical sometimes. But I know my colleagues, and we do not want to be hypocritical. Our employees, though, find us hypocritical when we say "don't worry, we will follow the rules, we will have fewer regulations and we will trust you more and we then will support you"; we have not solved this problem. The model should work very well in the public sector, but there are very practical reasons why it is not, and Phil Murray is trying to do so in the RCMP, despite newspaper critics.

Jacques Duchesneau: About management style, I would simply say that "small is beautiful." We have 5,700 employees, decentralized in forty-nine district offices. These are much smaller, without incarceration quarters. We think this more friendly administration makes people feel comfortable in going to police stations, because our best allies are the citizens. We aim to be a police service that is much closer to people.

Huguette Labelle: Administrating a department means a lot of different things. What I think is the most vital need of exploration is interface; the interface with other Canadian governmental organizations in order to help a horizontal integration of policy and process.

MANAGING ACTION: DO, ADVISE AND NEGOCIATE PUBLICLY

Participants saw three main action-tasks for public managers. They saw these action-tasks as inseparable and cautioned that these should be appropriately gauged to the manager's level in the bureaucratic hierarchy. First, participants agreed that managers must nurture themselves. It was agreed that a second action-task was negotiation and that it is intrinsic to the daily routine of the public manager. They cautioned that the craft of negotiating between articulate and well-defended social groups in a highly publicized environment while at the same time serving politicians (the third task) is indeed very demanding.

Huguette Labelle: Mintzberg wrote about an environment that pitted policy and management against each other. It was policy *versus* management. When I consider this expression in the context of the role of a deputy minister, I would not invoke "versus." This is a false debate; if we want the policy advice we are giving to be relevant, it must be based on the client perspective as well as on the perspective of first-line employees who deliver every day. What our employees do is deliver policy to the citizens. Of course, we must work with a political sensitivity and interact with the minister and other departments. I think we must be aware of those false debates, because we cannot deliver services, and we cannot propose a policy to a minister, if this product comes from a simply linear reflection. It is an integration that must be made constantly, and it is important that the deputy minister examine the interface between the employees and the public, even if we "work through the people around us," as Mintzberg writes.

Gérard Divay: Mintzberg's scheme is interesting with its concentric circles surrounding the manager at the centre; it reminds me of the eye of the tornado, where most of us are. Still, I would argue that the schema is missing a dimension. The role of the manager is, ultimately, to enrich the perspective. He or she is the one who receives all points of view separately and takes them into consideration in light of the others. When an official asks a very particular question, the role of a manager is to say: "OK, but have you thought of this or this impact?" It is the same with what comes from the administrative machine, especially with our very specialized organizations. I am under the impression that a great part of the manager's work is to organize people in order to study consequences and to discover interactions.

Cécile Cléroux: I would again emphasize that we are asked to do this publicly. Superior communication skills are increasingly required for managers. I would take it further: the public manager must now have the capacity to walk tightropes, to bear a costume, assume a role and all the decorum necessary to perform in public sessions. This act is obviously preceded by an insane sequence of telephone calls that will really slow the progression of the work. I have come to the conclusion that "democratic" management has been pushed to the threshold of paralysis by the need for transparency. Moreover, this wish for transparency has lost its sense of proportion, because in the context of this transparency, everybody has rights, but nobody has responsibilities. The interest groups' capacity to emphasize different interests often has totally distorted the issues. Management matters thus become very political and, in the long-term, work against the general interest.

Well-Rounded Job?

Participants stressed the importance of situational analysis either to adapt or to enrich the perspective in which decisions must be made. For the public manager to succeed, he or she must remain at the centre of the action and "in touch." The loss of policy capacity in the wake of fiscal cuts has put this critical endeavour at risk. Many governments have opted to eliminate or radically restructure public organizations without adequately assessing the wisdom of what amounted to superficial solutions that allowed little room for civil servants to manœuvre.

Pierre De Celles: I would insist on the adaptation that the administrator must often assume: the obligation to adapt his thought, his communication styles, his relationship with others. Therefore, this is not only an "interaction matter" for the manager, but also a question of increasing the adaptive potential of his organization. In this light, is there anything that particularly characterizes public administration? Where are, in this model, the differences between public and private management you are talking about? Are these different roles integrated differently? How do political constraints affect this reality? Or is it that within public administration, a particular style is used that has no equivalent in private enterprise? Finally, and at the risk of appearing a little presumptuous, I would suggest the following: rather than concentric circles as shown in the graph, wouldn't it be more interesting to have a "doughnut" where action would come from behind to join the core in an interaction, therefore, where the last layer would come from behind to interact with this core. I think this interaction is essential: it makes things progress, it transforms; the graph should, therefore, emphasize this.

Nicole Fontaine: We are living in a period in which many people have had to quit the public service, because of downsizing or retirement, thus depriving the organization of vital knowledge and memory. Earlier, it was said that we mostly kept the people who were "doing" the job; because of that, we now have a lot of "doers," and I wonder if we have a shortage of people who can re-think, who can ensure the necessary adaptation of an enterprise. All these cuts were made in accordance with a democratic wish, but I would argue that they were pushed to the limit by the media, consultants and political commitments. For all that, we had to maintain the saying: "Yes, yes, we are keeping the regional offices opened! Yes, we are keeping the client services, do not worry!" Personally, I am very worried, because the organizations may have lost most of their capacity to evolve, to adapt to an environment that is evolving very rapidly.

Henry Mintzberg: Continuous adaptation is interesting. Do we treat it as a role or do we treat it as goal of this instance? When I am talking about "frame," it refers to three meanings. One is to maintain the organization as a unit, as it is; this means "let's not move anything in case we make errors!" Adaptation is a little bit stronger, and change is stronger still.

A Role at Centre

Henry Mintzberg: Our view of organizations is like a chain, that is, one thing after the other. We follow a sequence. This is mass production, the assembly line. This means we quantify: first thing, second thing, third thing, etc. Often, organizations do not work as chains. In the production sector, we talk about "job shops." Job shops means that we have different machines and that each product flows through according to its own needs. We use the term "hub" for airline companies. Atlanta is a "hub" for Delta Air Lines. In a "hub," the manager is in the centre. Then there is the web, or network. Where is the manager in the network? This is an interesting question. I think the answer is, everywhere and nowhere. If the manager is not everywhere, he or she is nowhere. I followed a chief nurse in a Montreal hospital. She was "on the floor" all day. We met in her office early in the morning. First, she told me "I am practically never in this office; I spend the day on the floor." Partners of Morgan Stanley used to have their offices "on the floor." If you go back to *ménagement* and you go back to a household, to manage a house is to be on the floor. I mean, all good management is on the floor, and that includes the role of the deputy minister. If we want to manage a network, we must be everywhere. As for the hub, another detail comes from Sally Hegessen's *The Female Advantage, a Women's View of Leadership* (1990). She says that women do not describe themselves as being "on top," but rather as being in the middle, they are in the centre.

Roles to Balance: the Deputy's Case

Huguette Labelle: At one point, Mintzberg says "a good policy analyst may not be a good manager and vice versa," but I think that the example of the analysts is not isolated, and my experience really supports this statement. However, I think we must be careful and make a good distinction between the manager and the analyst. Of course, a deputy minister like John Tait is a super-analyst, but it is not his primary role. He must be many other things, as I recall Mintzberg's statement that the deputy minister is the one who arranges things so that what needs to be done is done. When we talk about the different roles of a deputy minister, I agree that the deputy minister is there to advise the minister on the development of policies, laws and regulations. He is also there to support the minister in his corporate role vis-à-vis the cabinet. In other words, for all the memoranda going to the cabinet and to the committees on which he sits, the minister expects support, even if the subject-matter is from a different sector.

The Evils of Structuritis

Huguette Labelle: However, when organizations are in a constant mutation, as it has been the case in the public sector and in the private sector over the last few years, people obviously do not know to whom they belong when they get up in the morning. Often, central agencies, who seem shielded from public demands for downsizing, have hoped for some magical solutions. A "fixer" looks good, because he or she triggers action at that moment, but government also requires "enlightened fixers," people who will take at least twenty-four hours to think about issues before finding a solution. Of course, sometimes we must make important changes or eliminate something completely, whether it is a unit within a department or a fusion of units, or even a division of units. We always wonder: "Why do we want to do this?" and "What is going to be different and better than what we have?" The turbulence of change, as well as the time consumed by change, sows confusion among the employees, and it may take several months and sometimes years before they can again visualize their position within the civil service. The costs in terms of people and services are probably much higher than we think. We must be careful. I think it could be very interesting to study the after-effects of the "structural movements." After my nomination at the Department of

Transport, I looked at the structural changes that had occurred in the twenty years before my arrival. At the end of the 1970s, the department had been reorganized to create administrations: air, surface, aeronautics, a small secretariat and a deputy minister. Managers were promised that each of these small administrations would be very autonomous. It did not take long before coordination, control and overlapping problems due to this reorganization were noticed, and they could not be solved easily. The department was again reorganized; it also had magical effects, but it also generated its own reform requirements.

Could Structure do it for Culture?

Henry Mintzberg: All internal and external pressures are interesting. They come from the press and electronic media, the political level, public servants, their unions, etc. There is an interesting story in England: They created an "executive agency" to manage prisons. They hired a high calibre corporate manager, a man who had been active in business. And he directed. Then there was a "break out": three people escaped. There was a scandal with a lot of pressure, revelations and questions in Parliament. The minister asked the head of the prisons to fire the chief warden of that prison, but he refused. So *he* went instead. When he left, he said they were more tightly controlled now as an executive agency than they were before. I find it interesting. This means that we can change anything we want on an organization chart, but we do not change as easily the spirit of the people.

Trapping Devices of Political Games

Henry Mintzberg: This is also a key example of the media influence. In the parliamentary system, Question Period is the best way in the world I know to raise problems and the worst way I know to solve problems. Our system is corrupted by "special interest groups" and money. It seems that since the beginning of my career, the presence of interest groups has increased. Money interests are much bigger now than they were before. In the United States, political action committees have emerged. It just makes public management harder. The "agencies" are a very logical idea for some things, but I am not sure this is the right solution. We will have to see the results. When we say "let the managers manage" and name somebody to be totally responsible for the results, it means centralization and not decentralization.

But the other thing is that the system is distorted in its fundamental design, because the more complicated the issue, the more management needs to be flexible and adaptable. You don't plan, but you react quickly, and you deal with the problems as they come up. Instead, we have this kind of childish notion of government: that there is administration and that there is politics. In other words, the politicians decide and the administrators act. And so you lock everything into legislation before you ever get a chance to test it. So it's not basically an adaptable system. By design, it's an inflexible system. The people at the bottom who could really make a difference cannot adapt very easily. Some people are sitting in Ottawa deciding without having to live with what is going on out there. I may not want civil servants – who are not voted in – making these decisions. But on the other hand, I don't want politicians controlling things they know nothing about.

MANAGING IN STYLE: ONE SIZE FITS ALL?

Managing publicly requires a particular character. It means taking into account public constraints and an individual's personal abilities to play the management game. Personal abilities invariably affect the managerial performance. The reverse is also true: Managerial constraints also affect personal abilities. Mintzberg identified different job frames in order to come to terms with it. Some job frames appear to be more directive, others place more emphasis on interpersonal relations and process.

John Tait: I appreciated Jacques Duchesneau's comments, and I will only add a few ideas to what he has said. First, I would like to talk about the day Mintzberg spent with Commissioner Norman Inkster. I have worked very closely with the RCMP for a long time, first when I was deputy solicitor general, but also when I was at Justice, and Inkster was a colleague during all this time. I have no doubt that the day they passed together was a representative day for Inkster. All the same, I think that if Mintzberg had visited Commissioner Phil Murray, who is now the commissioner, the day would have been similar and the impression would have been the same. But Phil Murray has a completely different management style; it is much more decentralized than Inkster's style.

I worked with Commissioner Simmonds, Inkster's predecessor. He was participating in operational decisions. Then, Inkster started to make things more flexible. He succeeded, I believe, although Murray has gone further in the same direction. His philosophy is to give people the ability and to make people responsible; he does not give a lot of directives. From what I can see, and I still work in the same field with him – as well as other fields – he has been successful.

Spending only a day with somebody can give you some idea of what he does, but there are limits to what it will reveal. Each leader in the RCMP, as in many other organizations, tries to find the right balance between two different factors. On one hand, we have the independence of a person (in this case the police officer) and the respect we have for this officer. At the other end of the scale is the requirement for leadership and conformity to policies and the law. With some distance, though, I see that we are always trying to find the appropriate balance for the moment rather than develop an approach that will be consistent.

Cécile Cléroux: Consequently, managing in such a context requires a very special disposition to be willing to commit; yes, there is a direct link between the personalities that we must seek and the type of management that we expect. For example, not all personalities can suffer stoically the personal criticism that is sometimes publicly directed to civil servants.

Henry Mintzberg: What has the most influence on the style and the role of the manager: the person or the context? Are there differences in this subject between the public and the private sector? The effect of the individual is his style, his personal approach, etc., while the effect of the context is the work, the organization, the unit, what there is to do. Personally, maybe because I am an engineer, I tend to lean on the instrumental style. I am not very postmodern. I believe that the context is more powerful than the person. Still, I do not want to say that one factor dominates the other. Obviously, it is always both. Perhaps there are styles that are determined, to a certain extent, by the work, the organization, the history.

RECRUITMENT, TRAINING AND SOCIALIZATION

Is the management of human resources in the public sector a distinct discipline? Is there a particular practice of public-sector management that is to be taught? Why are career paths so different? Could public-sector values be better taught in the public administration curricula, particularly in light of "new public management" practices? It is clear that criteria, selection and deployment of human resources are essential in transmitting visions into daily actions.

Pierre De Celles: Mintzberg's thoughts on roles are very interesting for those who are in the field of training managers or in the management of managers. Would it not be helpful to develop screening, evaluation and promotion mechanisms based on these types of skills that correspond to the roles, rather than being based on the traditional categories that have been used to this day? If the answer is yes, how are we going to develop the adequate descriptors, indicators and evaluation methods? I think this vision of the role of a manager will only be translated into reality when it will be taken into account during personnel screening, evaluation and promotion. Otherwise, there might be a rupture between the abstract understanding we have of the management reality and the way we determine the context and promote managers. In light of this, I would add that ÉNAP [the École nationale d'administration publique] must, of course, review some of its manager training methods.

Ralph Heintzman: This reminded me that a few years ago I had the occasion to read, almost simultaneously, two studies: one American and one Canadian. The first one showed that the percentage – I think it was around eighty or eighty-five per cent – of American CEOs came from the line rather than the staff. However, almost at the same time, I was reading a study made for us at the Canadian Centre for Management Development [CCMD] that showed that in the federal public service, close to the same percentage of deputy ministers came from the staff rather than from the line. This seems to show quite obviously that the "core competencies" in the public sector are not the same ones as in the private sector, and that, naturally, a system favours a particular kind of senior manager. Consequently, you are totally right to say that there is a series of things on which you put the emphasis on the public sector and there is another series that is valued in the other sector.

Daniel Maltais: Mintzberg's intention to define the differences between the private sector (non-profit and profit-making organizations) and the public sector (mainly non-profit-making organizations) is very interesting. On this point, even though I appreciated very much your description of the work of eight public managers, I am still wondering if there is a significant difference between what public-sector managers and private-sector managers do. In other words, what differences would we observe if we were comparing the daily work and concerns of these eight government managers with private-sector managers? If they were significant, would these differences modify the model or would they require that some elements of your model be enhanced? For example, many argue that the public manager, as a person, must have certain values such as a political neutrality, a consideration for public interest, a concern for transparency, an obligation to be reserved, etc. Of course, if we could agree on their importance in public management practices, these differences could contribute to the readjustment of current public management training programs, which, I think, imitate too often the "private" management.

Jacques Duchesneau: District policing is based on standardized organization control. First, in screening individuals, we go far beyond the résumé and now ask fundamental questions about values: why do you want to enter the police force? To help people? Perfect. This is the value and the attitude that must guide our future police officers – people who like people first. Today, thirty-five per cent of our new officers already have a university degree and this significantly changes the attitude. The second element is socialization – integrating our staff into the various communities. Essentially, the goal of the district office is to adapt to the local colour unlike before, when everything had to be the same.

SEMINAR CONCLUSION

Henry Mintzberg: I would like to thank you all for the enlightening and stimulating comments I have heard this afternoon. Your rich practical experiences have contributed to the development of my understanding of the roles of a public manager.

Among many things, I retain that while political life has changed a lot over the last few years, the political system has not developed as much. The role of the media, the pressures from interest groups, the citizens' expectations and public consultations, as well as the increasing complexity of public issues, are among the numerous factors that make the roles of public managers more and more difficult to perform. The political system and the "official" roles of public managers seem to have been created for situations that existed long before today, probably even in the last century. Because of this lack of adaptation, public managers must fit in a more artificial way in an extremely vast system, often quite detached from the concrete reality of the field. Of course, as Louis Bernard was saying, the separation of powers between ministers and deputy ministers should be considered again, as happened in the private sector, by separating the chair of the board from the position of president. Also, as suggested by Louis Bernard, ministers and deputy ministers' performance areas should be clarified in the field of administration and policy development.

Allow me to make a more general comment: the goal of my text was to trigger a debate from real cases and what I heard today is very encouraging because it prompted deep reactions from all participants. I was also impressed by the capacity of each one to illustrate from real situations some aspects of the model. Finally, I also noticed the great diversity of approaches used by the participants to deal with some aspects of the model. They have argued in favour of the enrichment of the model to take into account the complexity of the situations that a public manager must face.

NOTE

1 We gratefully acknowledge the editorial help of Patrice Dutil in writing this chapter.

6

Modelling the Public Manager: Is it Possible?

David Zussman
Jennifer Smith

In 1998, I was asked by the Institute of Public Administration of Canada and by the Canadian Centre for Management Development to contribute comments on a draft of Henry Mintzberg's "Managing Publicly." In response, Jennifer Smith and I have prepared the following comments on the Mintzberg model that are based on our experience and recent studies initiated through our work with the Public Management Research Centre (PMRC), the research arm of the Public Policy Forum.

Our research with the PMRC builds on survey data collected from managers in both the private and public sectors in 1986 and 1988 by David Zussman and Jak Jabes.[1] As well, much of the findings examined in this paper were gathered from recent focus group consultations with current and former executives and private-sector leaders. The results of this research indicate that the changing role of government makes it necessary for public managers to develop new competencies and work more closely with stakeholders and sectoral partners.

From our vantage point, Mintzberg's "Managing Publicly" does provide some pragmatic insight into managing in the public sector. Based on our research, however, it would seem that the model might be too static to accurately reflect the dynamic and constantly changing work environment that managers in the public sector face on a day-to-day basis.

Given the continual recasting of global dynamics, it makes sense that a model that worked less than five years ago would not be applicable in today's work environment, and one developed today would likely not be relevant in five years' time. The reality is, however, that the world is changing in the same ways for managers in all sectors of society. As a result, we are seeing a great deal more blurring of the lines between sectors and a need for managers to understand the world of their counterparts. This means that managers in the public sector are increasingly finding shared or common interests with private-sector managers. It does not mean, however, that the public sector must adopt the bottom-line focus of the private sector but rather requires a focus on "good" public administration and a public service that is well managed.

The work environment of today's public manager is increasingly complex. It needs to be determined whether a new model of managing in the public sector is evolving and, if so, what it looks like.

THE MODEL

In "Managing Publicly," Henry Mintzberg provides a model and examination of managerial work in the public sector. In essence, he has set out to capture the variety and flavour of managing in the public sector. Using his now well-known "diary" technique, Mintzberg observed a day-in-the-life of eight federal public servants at different levels of management, providing a fascinating glimpse into the complexity of issues and stakeholders that vie for a manager's time on a daily basis.

Mintzberg's model explains the core responsibilities of the public manager. The manager is shown to bring to the job his or her own values, knowledge and expertise that influence how the job is defined, how priorities are determined, and how strategies are developed, which are then manifested as management's agenda on specific issues.

According to the model, the work of public-sector managers takes place at three different levels, identified as information, people and action. First, the process, communication and control of information are seen as the most abstract level, whereby managers use available information to drive people towards a certain set of actions. At the second level, managing through people, managers are viewed as performing a leadership role on the individual, team and unit level, as well as providing a link between the internal world and the external community. Third, public managers manage dynamically by their own involvement in action, either by overseeing projects and "fighting fires" or by negotiating deals with players external to their unit.

All of these circles connect into Mintzberg's model of managerial work. The model is intended to demonstrate that all these components form one job and cannot be separated. And while these components may be separate parts of a job, Mintzberg contends that they cannot be separated behaviourally. It is recognized, however, that managers with different responsibilities and job-focuses will tend to emphasize some aspects of managing over others, depending on the agenda and the issues of the day.

Defining the job of the public-sector manager has been the source of great debate for many years. To paraphrase Thomas Teal, past editor of the *Harvard Business Review*, however, it would seem that managing cannot be summed up as a series of mechanical tasks nor can it be viewed simply as system interactions, because fundamentally it is a set of human interactions.[2] Essentially, it is this human element that requires more prominence in Mintzberg's model. Clearly, the human element is built into the model through the people level. However, Mintzberg's model does not appear to emphasize the fact that managing people needs to be a priority responsibility for managers, as is indicated by our research. This may result from the fact that the model is based on a snapshot of approximately twenty-nine managers, eight of whom are from the public sector, and examined in detail.

Mintzberg's case studies, therefore, may not necessarily reflect the day-to-day life of all public managers. As well, the lack of priority given to managing people is likely attributable to the fact that the model is more reflective of the current reality of being a public manager rather than the "optimal" model. While the case study of Norman Inkster, commissioner of the RCMP, does demonstrate the importance of developing organizational culture through people management, the reality is that the public-sector manager has many competing stakeholders, and often the political factors garner much of the public manager's attention. As often is the case, the urgent drives out the important. In essence, public managers work with their people to resolve issues of the day but spend less time actually managing their people.

REFLECTING ON THE PAST

Today what is clear is that there continues to be a constant struggle to create a federal public-service environment in which a manager can manage. Over the past seventy years, there have been five inquiries into the study of human resources in the federal public service. Sir Edward Beatty, Walter Gordon and Grant Glassco all headed up royal commissions, with perhaps the (Glassco) Royal Commission on Government Organization of 1962 being the most famous with its "let the managers manage" orientation. Following these studies were the 1979 (Lambert) Royal Commission Report on Financial Management and Accountability and the 1979 final report of the (D'Avignon) Special Committee on the Review of Personnel Management and the Merit Principle in the Public Service. All of these reported on issues and challenges faced by the federal public service in terms of human resources management and the identification of mechanisms required to ensure that prudence and probity are applied in the use of public expenditures. Some challenges identified by these commissions were unique to the times, while others were present throughout the twentieth century.

During the 1980s, a number of studies emerged that identified serious problems with underlying morale and evolving values of public servants in managerial positions. In 1986 and again in 1988, David Zussman and Jak Jabes surveyed a random selection of the senior management core and the executive cadre of the federal government to examine their attitudes towards the current management environment.[3] In addition, a sample of private-sector managers was also surveyed in order to compare the two sectors. The findings documented the many differences between public- and private-sector managers. It also found that over the two-year period there was a discernible weakening in public managerial perceptions and attitudes towards the current work environment, organizational culture, rewards and leadership practices.

One of the interesting findings of the study was the divergence of views across the management levels regarding managerial practices. In particular, it was found to exist that managers and senior managers do not share the same type of management experiences as those at the senior executive level. In addition, it was noted that managers at the lower levels do not have a shared sense of the "corporate culture," leadership, or the purpose and direction of the federal public service. This was largely attributed to the fact that lower-ranked managers had less access to information. As well, the concept of management within government focused on efficiency concerns and rules and process.[4] The authors concluded that the focus on rules and process promoted the development of managers who could develop system-based solutions to problems. From the authors' perspective, this "systems" style of management was viewed as the antithesis of good management. In fact, there was a fundamental conflict between the values associated with accountability and those that support originality, experimentation, inventiveness and risk-taking.

It was also noted that within the federal public service, a premium has been placed traditionally on policy development, with the responsibility of managing downward and administration often delegated to subordinates. Complicating this picture further is the degree to which managers are encouraged to undertake a series of interdepartmental movements as a means of moving up the ranks of the federal public service. This fact was noted in a recent study undertaken by the PMRC entitled *Today's Leaders: Career Trends of Canada's Private and Public Sector Executives*. For this study, individual federal agencies and departments were examined as if they were equivalent to private-sector organizations. As a result, deputy ministers (DMs), on average, moved through approximately five different departments before receiving their first DM appointment. Their

CEO counterparts, however, were more likely to be groomed up through the organization, only moving on average through one other organization before being appointed to their top position.[5]

As a result, almost seventy-five per cent of senior private-sector executives were appointed to their first CEO position from within their organization, compared to thirty-four per cent of their DM counterparts. Interestingly, senior executives in government tended to have a greater reliance on career moves through corporate or line functions rather than operations. In this sample, fifty-four per cent of the CEOs arrived at their top job with field or regional experience from outside the headquarters of their respective employer, compared to twenty-seven per cent of their public-sector counterparts.[6] Indeed, as noted by Peter Aucoin, since the 1970s there has been an increasing tendency for senior managers to be appointed to line departments in which they have no previous experience.[7] The consequence here is that DMs arrive at their new posting without any prior experience within the department.

The pattern of high career mobility among federal executives is based on the philosophy that senior leaders in the public sector require a broad understanding of the federal system, a wide variety of policy issues, and department/agency functions. In addition, it has been widely held that a more mobile executive and DM group would be more loyal to the government of the day than to their respective departments. In the private sector, senior leaders are far less mobile and generally are promoted to their position from within the ranks of their organization, having at one time or another lived the front-line.

TODAY'S EVOLVING ENVIRONMENT

It is evident that with the changes in the structure and size of government, a fundamental rethinking of its role has occurred. While there is increasing pressure for government to become more "business-like," the global trend appears to be moving societies towards becoming more "government-like," whereby the limited resources of government are focused on better policy development, with the devolution of service-delivery responsibilities to other levels of government or other sectors of the economy. In this evolving environment, what are the requirements and competencies for public managers?

Using the Mintzberg model, the requirements and competencies for public managers are essentially defined through the job frame. As the responsibilities of managers shift from service delivery to service management through devolution to other organizations, the purpose, perspective and position embodied by the job frame shift. Increasingly, managers are called to act as a bridge between the policy-makers within government and the service providers outside of government. The "communicating, linking and dealing" activities at the information, people and action levels become more and more prominent as the connection to entities outside of the government is strengthened.

In 1997, the PMRC met with approximately 130 federal executives from across Canada and approximately twenty-five former executives, within the National Capital Region, about a range of issues including work environment, their changing job, compensation and the challenges they face as public managers. As well, the PMRC met with twenty-four senior leaders and CEOs, twenty-nine senior vice-presidents of human resources, and eleven management consultants to discuss executive compensation and retention issues.

We have found that, in recent years, competencies for managers in both sectors have become increasingly similar. Given the changes confronting governments as they attempt to control public deficits, to respond to the new demands of the global, information society and to the escalating demands of its citizens, public managers have had to become familiar with traditional business concepts. This has led to significant changes in the nature of work in the public sector, and a greater emphasis is now placed on the costs and benefits of government services, with increased attention on the client and scrutiny of outcomes and results.

All of these factors, and particularly the movement towards adopting a more client-centerd focus and a commitment to a quality services framework, necessarily require skills that are more akin to those of private-sector managers. It is difficult to determine whether this is a trend that will continue in the future. However, we would predict that while there is a movement for the public sector to become more "government-like," it is clear that the taxpayer will continue to demand a greater voice in the decision-making process and more accountability for results. This will necessarily require the adoption of select business practices to the public sector while at the same time balancing the need to protect the public interest.

THE 1990s: THE TUMULTUOUS YEARS

In the 1990s, there have been significant changes in how the role of government is envisioned in Canadian society. In recent years, we have witnessed an increasing concern for annual deficits and the impact of a burgeoning national debt on Canadian competitiveness. As a result of a national focus on reducing the public debt, and the need to improve governance, the federal government introduced Program Review. At the broadest level, Program Review asked departments to assess their programs and redesign them to maintain their legal mandate but within the context of a steadily declining budget.

While deficit reduction was a primary objective of Program Review, it has also contributed to a widespread rethinking of the role of public services and public servants and has resulted in a shift in the culture of the federal public service. Today, departments and agencies are expected to apply the six guiding principles or questions of Program Review in determining resource allocation and program spending. In the end, Program Review generated significant departmental restructuring along resource lines, policy realignments, merging of service lines, and some significant downsizing. In December 1996, the population of the federal public service was 195,000, compared to 225,600 in April 1995. By the end of fiscal year 1997–98, the federal public service had been reduced by twenty per cent.

One of the primary outcomes of Program Review was a rethinking and transformation in the way federal programs and services are delivered. Today, managers are required to examine critically the need for federal involvement in the development and delivery of public programs and services. As a result, the federal government is, in many cases, entering partnership arrangements with other levels of government and other sectors of the economy. Through improved performance reporting to Parliament, the federal public service is also expected to ensure that the principles of effective and efficient use of public resources are maintained and improved where possible. These new requirements also have an impact on the types of skills required by today's public manager, leading to an increasing tendency to adopt private-sector practices and skills such as cost containment, decentralization, service and strategic realignment, greater reliance on alternative forms of service delivery, an openness to risk-taking, managing uncertainty and human capital, or "one's people," and a focus on outcomes and particularly the "client."

It is clear that the way the federal government discharges its roles and functions is changing significantly. Implicit in this argument is the recognition that federal public servants, as a result, have to operate under new realities, requirements and accountabilities. However, in a study recently conducted by the PMRC, *Final Report: Executive Consultations on Issues Related to Organizational Retention and Compensation*, it was found that the majority of federal executives consulted felt increasingly constrained by the human resources framework and the rules and processes that govern their current work environment.[8]

While acknowledging that there has been a fundamental rethinking in the role of government with the move towards more forms of alternative service delivery, federal executives feel they are still working in an unsettled environment in which their own ability to lead is challenged. From PMRC's consultations, it was concluded that it is imperative to have leaders in the public service who can inspire and communicate a vision to their staff. It was felt that the introduction of a long-term vision for the federal public service would enable executives to lead their groups in support of the overriding organizational vision. Today, managers in the federal public service tend to be looking for leadership from the top, not from within themselves. Instilling leadership in managers will be a difficult challenge within the public service, as managers continue to struggle, feeling they lack the appropriate direction to lead in their own units.

In recent PMRC consultations, managers also stated that the political factors are increasingly subsuming much of their day-to-day attention. What is unique to the public domain is the influence of politicians and the public on the work that is carried out by government, and increasingly the public is demanding more involvement in the decision-making process. As Canada moves to a more consultative form of governance, the public is more effectively leveraging the attention of ministers in order to address various concerns and issues. As a result, public servants are spending more and more time consulting clients and ministers during the course of their work. This was particularly the case in the regions where managers found they were increasingly expected to represent the federal government both within the community and with client and stakeholder groups as well. It was recognized by a number of executives in the National Capital Region that the distinction between serving the minister and serving the public had become increasingly blurred. This trend has had a substantial impact on the work environment surrounding public managers.

In a complementary study undertaken by the PMRC, entitled *Federal Executive Compensation and Retention: Perspectives from the Private Sector,* senior leaders in the private sector were asked to comment on issues related to executive compensation and retention in the federal public service. The majority of these leaders speculated that a number of the current problems confronting the federal public service could be attributed to the conflicting demands on the time and energy of those at the senior-most levels of government. In fact, a number of CEOs hypothesized that DMs today spend a substantial amount of their time managing the political aspects of their jobs (responding to the needs of the minister and his or her political staff).[9] As a result, the responsibility for managing the department becomes subordinate to the need to manage the political realities.

Many wondered how often DMs place people management as their highest priority. Further still, how often do DMs meet with their executive group as a team and ask tough questions, such as asking their managers whether things are being done the "right way," if there are any ideas of how something could be done better, what is impeding the managers or bothering them in their jobs or in their roles as federal executives? Mintzberg defines these activities as the "people" aspect of managerial work. In developing a 1997 article, Jacques Bourgault interviewed twenty-one federal DMs in order to understand better how these senior public servants manage their organization. In this study, it was found that DMs spend approximately nineteen per cent of their time meeting with immediate subordinates, compared to sixteen per cent on crisis management and fifteen per cent on human resources management.[10] In the private sector, CEOs we interviewed estimated that they spent in excess of fifty per cent of their time managing their people. It was emphasized that an important aspect of any senior leader's job is management (reaching beyond financial management to include people management). This aspect of managing and valuing people needs to be emphasized throughout all levels of the organization.

For managers, there are a number of consequences from spending increasing amounts of time attending to their ministers. In these cases, the management of the department and its people tends to get pushed to the backburner by the hotter, political issues of the day. Peter Aucoin provides a number of examples from both within and outside Canada of what can go wrong when top officials and subsequently their managers "focus their efforts on serving the interests of ministers to the detriment of their leadership of the public service," with the Al-Mashat affair in Canada being one of the most extreme case cited.[11] While the examples given focus on the most senior levels of government, it is clear from our studies that managers take their sense of direction and priorities from signals given from above. Senior managers are often criticized by employees for tending to the directives from ministers or central agencies, over the needs of the department.

Clearly, a great deal of a public manager's time is spent putting out fires and managing issues rather than people. This factor alone detracts from a public manager's ability to manage beyond a short-term horizon and to factor in the impact decisions and changing directions have on staff morale and organizational commitment. Indeed, the mere position titles of senior public leaders reflect the primary emphasis of the position. The titles "deputy minister" and "assistant deputy minister" indicate that these positions are focused on managing the political aspects of the job.

New Zealand, Australia and the United Kingdom have seen a movement away from the traditional Westminster model to the development of executive agencies or special operating enterprises that effectively separate the policy from the service-delivery aspect. The heads of these agencies are generally given the title of "chief executive officer" to reflect their accountability and responsibility to lead the organization and deliver public services. In theory, policy advice is left to ministerial advisers, although we recognize that in practice this is not always the case. Similar trends can be found in the private sector. For example, Nova Chemicals has changed the title of their senior executives within human resources to more closely reflect the people culture they are attempting to foster. Previous positions that were titled vice-president of human resources or personnel have been renamed "vice-president people."

Given this changing environment and the new requirements for today's public managers, one must question whether managers at all levels can realistically allocate appropriate time to people management or if the political realities of the job always prevail. In many organizations, the chief executive officer has little time to oversee the people management of the organization. As a result, a number of companies have centralized the human resources (HR) function, ensuring that the vice-president of HR is part of the senior executive management committee. This allows for senior leaders to focus on the strategic leadership of the organization, while ensuring that the responsibilities for the people component of managing are undertaken. The strategic repositioning of the HR function in the private sector, therefore, has led to greater accountability for people leadership by ensuring integration between operations and people management.

In the public sector, there exists a different attitude towards people management that is largely driven by more formalized processes and functional stovepipes. In the federal government, the HR function is very decentralized, and responsibility for human resources management falls on a number of central agencies, *as well as* the heads of personnel, renewal council, and the committee of senior officials. The HR community is diffused across departments and as a result the degree to which line managers are held accountable for their people management responsibilities is often dependent on individual deputy ministers.

REQUIREMENTS FOR TODAY'S PUBLIC MANAGER

Similar to the private sector, the job of managing in the public sector requires that managers acquire traditional managerial skills including finance, budgeting, resource allocation, cost control and risk management. As Teal points out, however, these skills are in abundance as universities churn out graduates from multidisciplinary studies such as commerce, business and public administration. In essence, individuals with these skills can easily be found in the marketplace. The challenge in the public sector is balancing the need to understand the broader policy environment, its political implications, and the notion of the public interest, with the need to lead an organization.

As noted by Teal, what is perhaps more difficult is instilling in managers the human element of management – teaching people to truly behave like managers.[12] What is required is to instal and develop new management competencies such as leadership, communication, strategy, vision, ethical standards, accountability, citizen engagement, integrity and character. Interestingly, these competencies can be rearranged within Mintzberg's model of managerial work: the job frame embodies strategy, vision and ethical standards; communication, accountability and citizen engagement fall under information; the people level includes leadership and ethical standards; and action embraces integrity and character. These critical elements are increasingly a management requirement – skills that often cannot be acquired through a traditional educational track. These skills can only be acquired through experiential learning such as formal and informal personal development, mentoring, acting positions, secondments and intersectoral exchange programs. All of these promote improved understanding and communication between managers in all sectors.

We would suggest that the human element of management is fundamentally missing within the federal government. Rather, managers tend to be promoted based on technical competencies. Being a good policy adviser, scientist or engineer does not necessarily mean that one will also be a good manager. As noted by Aucoin, Canada, following in the Westminster model, has generally promoted managers to senior federal public service positions based on policy-related rather than operational experience.[13] (An example of this occurrence can be identified through the case study on John Tait within the Mintzberg analysis.) As a result, senior managers often are more adept at managing the policy process than managing the operations and people in an organization.

CONCLUSION

The call of the Glassco Commission to let the managers manage continues to be relevant. Equally important today, however, is teaching and instilling in people the ability to act and behave like people managers. Clearly, promoting people into management positions based on technical or policy expertise is no longer a viable practice. Based on our research findings, we would say that managers who have strong leadership abilities, who are strategic, who can communicate a vision and inspire their people to follow a desired direction will succeed in the new millennium. In light of the political realities of a public manager, however, can all managers in government be expected to focus a sufficient amount of their time on their people? Our research would indicate that, at the most senior levels, close attention to people management is a challenge. As a result, a more centralized approach to human resources management can only help to support DMs in the management of their organizations. With this being said, true leaders cannot lose sight of the factors that are key to long-term success.

It is recognized, increasingly, in the private sector that success in a global economy depends to a great extent on people. In essence, it is now clearly understood that providing good customer service and products is the direct result of managing people well. As a result, a highly motivated and well-directed workforce is viewed as one of the critical tasks of managers. Our research findings indicate that this aspect needs greater emphasis within Mintzberg's model of managerial work. Although we recognize that managing people, not issues and processes through people, was not a prominent aspect of the day-to-day reality found in the individual case studies used in the development of the Mintzberg model. In a sense, the model may be an accurate reflection of the daily reality, but it may not be the optimal model for public managers.

The question remains whether management in the public sector should more closely reflect management practices in the private sector. In 1994, Harold Grover recommended that future executives in government become "leaders by design," thereby benefiting from career development that models "great entrepreneurs."[14] Others, including Henry Mintzberg, take great exception to this statement, arguing that the fundamental purpose of the public service is to serve the public interest, which necessarily dictates that private-sector, bottom-line expectations should not be applied to government.

The debate of whether public-sector managers should more closely emulate the background, experience and business practices of their private-sector counterparts continues. In reality, what is clear is that good administration practices are required in organizations across all sectors. Organizations, whether they belong in the public, private or third sector, need to be managed well to succeed. The model of the late 1980s and early 1990s of the "leaner and meaner" organization is being fundamentally challenged in a global economy. Today many companies view their people as their most valuable asset – intellectual capital is perceived to be the competitive advantage of the twenty-first century. Innovation and a strong client orientation can only be fostered in an environment that has strong leadership and that values its people. In the end, good managers don't manage systems, they manage people.

NOTES

1 David Zussman and Jak Jabes, *The Vertical Solitude: Managing in the Public Sector* (Montreal: Institute for Research on Public Policy, 1989).
2 Thomas Teal, "The human side of management," *Harvard Business Review* 74, no. 6 (November/December 1996), p. 36.
3 Zussman and Jabes, *Vertical Solitude.*
4 Ibid.
5 Sharon Varette and David Zussman, *Today's Leaders: Career Trends of Canada's Private and Public Sector Executives* (Ottawa: Public Management Research Centre, 1996), p. 10.
6 Ibid., p. 11.
7 Peter Aucoin, *The New Public Management: Canada in Comparative Perspective* (Montreal: Institute for Research on Public Policy, 1995), p. 67.
8 David Zussman, Jennifer Smith and S. Snider, *Final Report: Executive Consultations on Issues Related to Organizational Retention and Compensation* (Ottawa: Public Management Research Centre, 1997).
9 David Zussman, Jennifer Smith and S. Snider, *Federal Executive Compensation and Retention: Perspectives from the Private Sector* (Ottawa: Public Management Research Centre, 1997), p. 22.
10 Jacques Bourgault, "De Kafka au Net : la lutte de tous les instants pour le contrôle de l'agenda chez les sous-ministres canadiens," *Gestion* 22, no. 2 (June 1997), pp. 18–26.
11 Aucoin, *New Public Management*, p. 64.
12 Teal, "The human side of management," *Harvard Business Review,* p. 36.
13 Aucoin, *New Public Management*, p. 65.
14 Harold L. Grover, "Transition leadership and legacies," *Public Manager* 23, no. 2 (Summer 1994), pp. 13–16.

7

Executive Management in the Public Sector: Some Observations

Mohamed Charih

WHAT DO MANAGERS DO?

Practitioners and academics have been trying to answer the question of what managers do since the turn of the last century. Henri Fayol was the first to identify and articulate the functions of managers. He said that their functions are to forecast, organize, coordinate, command and control. In saying this, Fayol and his disciples, such as Luther Gulick and Lyndall F. Urwick, not only identified the functions of managers but made it possible for management to be taught as a subject.[1] For many decades the function-oriented approach to management was the predominant perspective for understanding, practising and teaching management.

Under function-oriented management, executive management must play a pre-eminent role in planning. Management must follow and interpret the general trends in the external environment, monitor changes in the economic, political and social situation, and identify new issues and new opportunities. Through the analysis and interpretation of environmental factors, executive management places the organization within its environment by defining its mission, its objectives, and strategic methods of achieving those objectives. Translation of strategic orientations into concrete activities, organization and direction are left to the middle and first-line managers. Control has often been divided into strategic control, which is a counterpart of planning, and operational control, which is generally the responsibility of the middle and first-line managers.

Despite its undeniable contribution to the study of management and its popularity, the function-oriented approach to management had its detractors, the most important of them being H.A. Simon.[2] For Simon, the function-based approach, including its underlying administrative principles, lacks coherence, rigour and logic. It is not clear whether its prescriptions constitute proposals that have been tested or hypotheses in search of empirical confirmation. In short, Simon did not hesitate to refer to the principles underlying this management approach as management proverbs.

In the early 1970s, Henry Mintzberg made an important contribution to the study of managers' roles.[3] By observing executives in action, he carried out an original research project on the nature of managerial work. This gave birth to a perspective based on roles rather than functions. Going beyond what he termed the folklore (i.e., planning, organizing, directing and controlling), Mintzberg suggested that there are ten roles that managers assume in their work: three are interpersonal, three informational, and four decisional.

One of Mintzberg's most important contributions was to position the manager at the centre of the management process in general and of the life of the organization in particular. The role-oriented perspective taught us that the manager's work is at once complex and highly varied. This perspective offered a more detailed explanation than did the function-based approach of the different hats that a manager might wear, depending on the organizational context, the nature of the organization's business, and position in the hierarchy. This focus on the roles of managers enjoyed unprecedented dissemination throughout the world and today still remains very popular with academics and practitioners alike.

Furthermore, the focus on roles has served to enhance the teaching of management in management schools and has opened the door to the development of new courses such as negotiation and dispute resolution. This is not to say that the aspects in question were totally absent from the instruction of function-oriented management, but rather that examination of management on the basis of roles directed attention towards certain new skills that must also be mastered by managers.

While Mintzberg's study looked at the roles of various types of managers and directors (general and shop foremen, functional managers, sales directors, hospital administrators, corporation presidents, even heads of state), a more thorough examination of the roles of managers in a parliamentary public administration still remained to be done, until now.

WHAT DO PUBLIC MANAGERS DO?

In Canada, this question has not received the attention it deserves, whether from academics or royal commissions, even though the Boudreau Commission in Quebec (1993) and the Public Service Commission of Canada (1993) have made an effort.[4] Generally, it has often been assumed that the functions and roles of public managers are similar if not identical to those of their counterparts in the private sector. Adopting this perspective, the (Glassco) Royal Commission on Government Organization (1962) recommended that the federal government "let the manager manage," and the (Lambert) Royal Commission on Financial Management and Accountability (1979), that it "require the manager to manage."[5] In order to promote management, the Lambert Commission proposed separating political responsibility from administrative responsibility, assigning the former to the minister and the latter to the deputy minister. Influenced by the role of managers in the private sector, Glassco and Lambert did not concern themselves with defining the management responsibilities of public servants in a parliamentary system. The politicians saw this concept as a usurpation of their power: they and the senior officials of the central agencies were opposed to this transformation of the role of public servant/adviser into manager, especially since it was one that neither Glassco nor Lambert had bothered to legitimize.[6]

In this connection, former secretary of the Treasury Board, Al Johnson, comments as follows:

> The heart of the failure [of the proposed new management regimes], as I see it, was that the advocates of the comprehensive reforms did not adequately cope with the question of how the reforms would "fit" in parliamentary government. ... How can reform be made workable in the political environment that government operates in, when every exercise of responsibility, and every answer in the name of accountability, is judged in political terms?[7]

What is more, the administrations of Canadian prime ministers Lester Pearson, Pierre Trudeau and Joe Clark endeavoured to transfer the important decisions from the bureaucrats to the cabinet. For example, the Policy and Expenditure Management System, introduced to the federal government in 1979, was designed to integrate policy development and resource allocation. Concurrently with this centralization of important decisions within the cabinet and central agencies, we also saw increasing participation by senior officials in public policy development, rendering the boundary line between politics and administration ever more hazy.

Starting in the mid-1980s, the context of public management went through a number of changes. Like England, the United States, Australia and New Zealand, Canada undertook certain reforms based on the "new public management."[8] This new trend of public management seeks to redefine the role of the state, eliminate the deficit, separate policy from operations, introduce management by results, grant managers increased powers, and put the emphasis on satisfying client needs. As for the means of accomplishing this, the government has to invent new organizational forms of service delivery such as privatization, contracting-out, partnerships and the commercialization of public services.[9] The loss of confidence in public institutions, crises in public finances, evolution of the information technologies, demands of globalization and the rise of the "new right" modelled on the public choice school and the agency perspective are at the source of reforms such as the Program Review of 1984, the adoption of special operating agencies (1989), Public Service 2000 (1990) and the Program Review of 1994–95.

Basically, the reforms issuing from the new public management were designed to strengthen the role of strategic management by the political level and to restore a balance of power within cabinet in order to promote disciplined strategic direction of public policy management and the devolution of implementation, with the aim of ensuring that public programs and services perform better. In this process, the balance of power is shifted in two directions at once, to use Aucoin's expression.[10] In this context, the political realm and the bureaucratic realm become blurred, relations with the administrative level call out for redefinition, and the foundations and conventions of a parliamentary public administration, such as collective cabinet responsibility, ministerial responsibility, public-servant anonymity, and political neutrality, are open to challenge and questioning.[11] In this regard, alternative models of public-service delivery, such as special operating agencies, consultations conducted by government officials, and media pressure for public-servant accountability, contribute on the one hand to reducing the scope of ministerial responsibility and on the other to gradually making anonymity and political neutrality difficult to maintain.

The advent of new public management, which would separate policy development ("steering") from operations ("rowing"), has also led to a revival of the old debate on the relevance of the distinction between the politics and the administration. Whether or not one is in agreement on the formative consequences of separating policy development from operations on the management responsibilities and powers of politicians, as compared with those of public servants, the prerequisite is first of all to define the role of public managers and secondly to legitimize it. Recently a federal deputy minister task force examined the definition of the roles and responsibilities of public servants relative to those of politicians.[12] In this context, a study of the various roles of managers in a parliamentary public administration constitutes an interesting contribution to this debate.

A PUBLIC MANAGEMENT MODEL

Mintzberg's study is a first step in the right direction. In my opinion, it opens the door to systematic research on a management model specific to the public sector and, above all, in a parliamentary public administration. Some major public administration reforms have come up against some major obstacles because we have no model to define and legitimize the roles of public managers as opposed to those of politicians.

The first important contribution of Mintzberg's research is to examine the roles of managers in the context of government administration. His exploration of the roles of eight public managers in action has shown how public dimensions ("publicness"), the nature of the department or agency, hierarchical position, frame of reference, and nature of the activity to be carried out affect the roles of public managers. This study paves the way for research on the roles of public managers in different contexts and on comparisons between the public and private sectors.

At the heart of this conceptual model we find the concept of the framework of action and the setting of the agenda. Whether senior or newly appointed, the manager brings with him in the exercise of the management function a complex of knowledge, beliefs and values. Taking account of the contingencies peculiar to the organization and to the position occupied helps the manager delimit his or her arena of action and develop intervention and management strategies. Empirical studies indicate that effective managers spend a good deal of their time in understanding the context in which they must work, defining issues, and drawing up their target agenda of achievements.[13]

PUBLIC MANAGEMENT MODELS

Henry Mintzberg tested his conceptual model in three different federal public organizations: Parks Canada, the Royal Canadian Mounted Police, and the Department of Justice. Upon completing this test, he identified three models of public management: the managing on the edges model, the cultural management model, and the policy management model. While these different models are not in my view mutually exclusive, they each have certain distinctive characteristics.

The Managing on the Edges Model

The context of managing on the edges is very interesting. It clearly shows that, while it is not easy in practice to separate policy development from management, separating management from politics (including partisan politics) is a real challenge in the public sector. The case of Parks Canada is eloquent in this regard. Here the trees and greenery conceal a dynamic of different players with diverging interests, leading to the politicization of management issues. In the process, matters that ought initially to be the business of management are transferred to the headquarters in Ottawa, where they mobilize senior officials and politicians. A second method of appropriating what would seem to be the business of management structures is recourse to the courts by citizens, interest groups, and even other levels of government to argue against managerial decisions. This may seem abnormal to a management specialist, but for a political scientist or sociologist of power it is democracy in action.

This situation led the regional Parks Canada director to assign an important role to "linking," particularly with the head office in Ottawa. In my view, it is quite clear that this case stands as an excellent illustration of how the political context of public administration affects the frame of reference of the regional director, her intervention strategies and her management style. How much of this behaviour can be attributed to personality remains to be determined.

The managing on the edges model, especially in a politically sensitive context, involves managing up via communication and linking with Ottawa. The monitoring of changes in the frame of reference at headquarters and in political imperatives serves to keep Parks management in line with the expectations of the political level and hence to meet the requirements of ministerial responsibility, a key element of parliamentary democracy. But excessive managing up does not necessarily guarantee the long-term effectiveness of the organization. It has to be balanced by managing out and managing down. The former helps senior managers keep an eye on the demands and expectations of the various players concerned with the organization's activities, and the latter serves to realize its objectives. The managing on the edges model can in fact be considered as a general management model.

The Cultural Management Model

The cultural management model, found at the Royal Canadian Mounted Police, gives the creation and introduction of an organizational culture priority over the other management roles. Such a culture, reinforced by leadership and communication, fills in for and in certain cases minimizes the importance of traditional controls. The organizational structure then assumes the shape of a circle, where executive management is at the centre and not the top. The success of this model is based, on the one hand, on a new way of conceiving organizational management and, on the other, on the selection of candidates who have the appropriate values and attitudes, the presence of an integrating system of socialization, management by principles, and shared responsibility. The main reasons why this model has not become widespread are that establishing a culture demands a good deal of time and great stability in executive management, the recruiting of persons who have the profile and attitudes sought, and training and socialization by training centres or schools affiliated with the organization.

While organizational culture and values have held an important place in public and private organizations since the early eighties, the reforms driven by the rhetoric of new public management have introduced into public administration new values that have largely been borrowed from the private sector. To the traditional values of public administration such as political responsibility, integrity, equity and neutrality have been added entrepreneurship, excellence, quality service and innovation.[14] The federal Deputy Minister's Task Force on Public Service Values and Ethics has noted this new constellation of values as a source of various tensions in the management of public affairs:

> [V]alues discourse in the public service (and in other organizations) has not been sufficiently clear and forthright about conflicts between values. We are inclined to think that value conflicts arise only between our values and their opposites. We are not sufficiently alive to what the philosophers call the hierarchy of values, to the fact that our values conflict not only with their opposites but with each other.[15]

Management via a cultural model involves two things: first, a clarification and commitment by the public organization with regard to the values to be promoted, plus a fairly stable management environment; and, second, a managerial capacity to instil the values adopted and arbitrate between them, plus a system of socialization that can communicate and uphold them.

The Public Policy Management Model

Policy analysis and development is the central concern of the public policy management model. At the Department of Justice, where this model was identified, managing up is the rule, given that the review and promulgation of new legislation require the approval of politicians and parliamentarians. Managing down, while not paramount, is also vital for achieving the objectives of the department and providing it with the appropriate management systems and skills.

Whereas the managing on the edges model focuses more on the different facets of public management – managing up, managing down, managing out – the policy management model partakes more of the traditional concept of executive management in public administration, which was supposed to provide public policy advice to the political level.

This is a model of high political involvement compared with the managing on the edges model or with the cultural management model where the involvement of politicians is relatively minimal. Because this model assigns secondary importance to managing down, it provides fuel for the critics who argue that the public executive ascribes more importance to political advice, to the detriment of management.[16] It is important however to note that the place occupied by policy evaluation and development in executive management activities varies according to the mandate of the department or agency concerned. Whereas policy development has not suffered much in recent years at the Department of Justice, for the federal government as a whole, certain steps have been taken to restore new vigour to this function.

WHAT DO THE LEADERS OF PUBLIC AFFAIRS DO?

It is essential to understand the roles and responsibilities of public managers. But it is also fundamental, in a general model of public management, to define the roles, responsibilities and behaviour of the leaders of public affairs, that is, the politicians and especially the ministers. Donald Savoie has identified four orientations common to ministers: status, mission, policy and processes. Status-oriented ministers are mainly concerned about their visibility, while the mission-oriented are obsessed with getting their projects adopted and implemented. Policy-oriented ministers strive to influence and shape certain public policies in which they have expertise. Policy content, organization and management matters are of little concern to process-oriented ministers, who juggle with the various processes they control in order to obtain advantages for their clientele or their constituency.[17] The issue of ministerial orientations leads us to at least two questions. How does the minister's style in managing public affairs affect the frame of reference and room to manœuvre of the department's executive management? And how do managing up, managing down and managing out function under the different ministerial orientations?

CONCLUSION

As mentioned earlier, Henry Mintzberg's work paves the way for studies on the roles of managers in the public sector. But the conceptual model initially employed in this research is not sufficiently specific to the public sector. Kenneth Kernaghan and I have already issued an appeal in this regard.[18] In an analysis of emerging issues in contemporary public administration, produced on the occasion of the fiftieth anniversary of the

Institute of Public Administration of Canada, we recommended that a model of public management be developed that is anchored in public law, political science and management science. In this process, a viable model of public management must also incorporate politicians and their roles and highlight how their roles converge with and differ from those of bureaucrats or public servants.

In the private sector, the type and logic of the industry, the strategies of the competition, and the previous strategies of the organization are among the parameters that determine the frame of reference for the manager's action. In the public sector, organizations are governed by the political will to fill certain mandates in various fields in the public interest. In that context, managers must come to terms with the sovereignty of Parliament, ministerial responsibility and solidarity, and the program of the party in power. The frame of reference of public managers and how much room they have to manœuvre are therefore contingent on political imperatives, the departmental or organizational mandate, and the distribution of power among the various departments and agencies and the different levels of government.

What do the leaders of public affairs – that is, the politicians and in particular the ministers – do? How do ministers define their own frame of reference? How do they establish orientations for their portfolio? How do they instil their vision within the department? How do they hold their employees accountable? How does the minister's management style affect the executive management style of the department?

NOTES

1 Henri Fayol, *Administration industrielle et générale*, new edition (Paris: Dunod, 1999); Luther Gulick and Lyndall F. Urwick, *Papers on the Science of Administration* (New York: Columbia University Press, 1937).

2 H.A. Simon, *Administrative Behavior: A Study of Decision-Making Process in Organizations* (New York: The Free Press, 1947).

3 Henry Mintzberg, *The Nature of Managerial Work* (New York: Harper & Row, 1973).

4 Quebec, Commission concernant la préparation de la relève des gestionnaires pour la fonction publique québécoise, *Rapport* (Hull: École nationale d'administration publique, 1993); Canada, Public Service Commission, *Profil des leaders et gestionnaires de la fonction publique* (Ottawa: Commission, 1993).

5 Canada, Royal Commission on Government Organization [Glassco Commission], *Management of the Public Service* (Ottawa: Queen's Printer, 1962); Canada, Royal Commission on Financial Management and Accountability [Lambert Commission], *Final Report* (Ottawa: Supply and Services Canada, 1979).

6 Mohamed Charih, "Le management du troisième type au gouvernement fédéral," in R. Parenteau, ed., *Le Management Public* (Ste-Foy: Presses de l'Université du Québec, 1992).
7 A.W. Johnson, *Réflexions sur la réforme de l'administration fédérale du Canada* (Ottawa: Office of the Auditor General, 1992), p. 16.
8 Peter Aucoin, *The New Public Management: Canada in Comparative Perspective* (Montreal: Institute for Research on Public Policy, 1995); Mohamed Charih and Lucie Rouillard, "The New Public Management," in Mohamed Charih and Arthur Daniels, eds., *New Public Management and Public Administration in Canada*. Monographs in Canadian Public Administration – No. 20 (Toronto and Hull: Institute of Public Administration and École nationale d'administration publique, 1997), pp. 27–45.
9 Canada, Privy Council Office, Public Service 2000, *The Renewal of the Public Service* (Ottawa: Supply and Services Canada, 1990); Aucoin, *New Public Management*; David Osborne and Ted Gaebler, *Reinventing Government: How the Entrepreneurial Spirit is Transforming the Public Sector From Schoolhouse to State House, City Hall to Pentagon* (Reading, Mass.: Addison-Wesley, 1992).
10 Aucoin, *New Public Management*, p. 4.
11 Paul G. Thomas, "Ministerial Responsibility and Administrative Accountability," in Charih and Daniels, *New Public Management*; Kenneth Kernaghan and Mohamed Charih, "The challenges of change: emerging issues in contemporary public administration," CANADIAN PUBLIC ADMINISTRATION 40, no. 2 (Summer 1997), pp. 218–33.
12 Canada, Deputy Minister's Task Force on Public Service Values and Ethics, *Discussion Paper* (Ottawa: Privy Council Office, 1996).
13 J.P. Kotter, *The General Manager* (New York: The Free Press, 1982); Robert D. Behn, "Branch Rickey as public manager: fulfilling the eight responsibilities of public management," *Journal of Public Administration Research and Theory* 7, no. 1 (June 1997), pp. 1–33.
14 Kenneth Kernaghan, "Shaking the Foundation: New versus Traditional Public-Service Values," in Charih and Daniels, *New Public Management*, pp. 47–65; Charih and Rouillard, "New Public Management," in Ibid.
15 Canada, Deputy Minister's Task Force on Public Service Values and Ethics, *Discussion Paper*, pp. 2–3.
16 Canada, Royal Commission on Financial Management and Accountability [Lambert Commission], *Final Report*.
17 Donald J. Savoie, *The Politics of Public Spending in Canada* (Toronto: University of Toronto Press, 1990), pp. 189–94.
18 Kernaghan and Charih, "The challenges of change: emerging issues in contemporary public administration," CANADIAN PUBLIC ADMINISTRATION.

8

Mintzberg on Public Management: The Wider Theoretical Debate

Paul G. Thomas

This chapter seeks to place Professor Mintzberg's recent work on public management in the context of the intellectual evolution of the field of public administration and the most recent debates over the ideas for public-service reform represented by the "new public management" (NPM) and reinventing government movements. A brief historical overview of organizational theory as it has been applied to the public sector is presented first to make the point that a great deal of what is said to be new in today's public management is actually old wine in new bottles. For example, the politics versus administration dichotomy from the earliest public administration literature is resurrected in the distinction of "steering" (policy) versus "rowing" (operations) in the contemporary reinventing government literature. Other ideas that had previously been tried and found wanting, often in the private sector, are now being applied in the public sector with a fervour and confidence that is unjustified given their past record and the distinctive challenges involved with "managing publicly" today.

The chapter then turns to an analysis and assessment of Professor Mintzberg's model of the behaviour of public managers. While praising the Mintzberg paper for providing a rich, complex and nuanced description of the real world of public managers, this chapter also seeks to raise some questions about the interpretative framework he applies. The chapter concludes that if we are to represent organizational reality and managerial activity in all its complexity, scholars are going to have to observe and listen to managers more closely. Equally important, academics will have to discover or invent language and concepts that are understandable and resonate with people who serve in government. Only then will we produce "practical theory" defined as theory that "either illuminates possibilities for action that would otherwise not be apparent or stimulates greater understanding of what the person has already been doing."[1]

ORGANIZATIONAL THEORY

During the past three decades we have acquired considerable empirical information on the types of activities in which managers engage on a daily basis. Largely through the research and integrative efforts of Professor Henry Mintzberg, many of the conventional assumptions about the nature of managerial work have been challenged and largely dispelled. Contrary to the popular stereotype, managers are not systematic planners who rely on carefully gathered intelligence, in-depth analysis and reflective decision-making to make strategic decisions about the future of their organizations. Instead, managerial life and work is seen to be multidimensional, complicated, information-rich, episodic, disjointed, value-laden and conflictual. Intuitive decision-making based on soft information predominates over scientific, rational approaches. In practice, strategic improvization often prevails over formal strategic planning. Instead of detailed blueprints in the form of plans to be followed unswervingly, it is the indirect benefits of planning that are most important to organizational success. Such benefits include better problem definition, improved communication, greater organizational coherence, the promotion of organizational and individual learning and improved motivation. In government, most innovations of any significance combine formal planning with what Robert Behn calls "management by groping along."[2]

Professor Mintzberg's earlier work focused mainly on decision-making in private firms, as opposed to public organizations. It is a welcome development that he has turned his attention to management tasks and activities in the public sector and even more encouraging is his recognition that there are distinctive challenges and constraints involved with "managing publicly" in contrast to managing privately.[3] Throughout the relatively short history of public administration as a field of study and practice, various commentators have drawn heavily on the ideas, models and techniques that were favoured at the time in the corporate sector. This was true even when the proponents of such approaches had first-hand experience working in government and might have been expected to recognize differences with the corporate sector. Instead, the prevailing assumption of the early organizational theorists was that scientific principles of good management were out there to be discovered and that they applied to all types of organizations. In addition to theories of scientific management, considerable faith was also placed in simple lists of structural principles and managerial practices. In other words, core managerial activities like planning, deciding, budgeting and human resource management could be conducted in basically the same way in all organizations.

Under the "generic" approach, little attention was paid to the distinctive context in which management processes operated in the public sector. In particular, the relationship between the political arm of government and the public service did not receive any special attention. Nor was any great emphasis placed on the distinctive tasks, environments, structures, procedures, outputs and outcomes that seem to differentiate public organizations from private firms. Downplaying such distinctions, the generic approach stressed that management's role in all organizations was to get things done in the most economical, efficient and effective manner possible. To achieve this outcome it was imperative that, as much as possible, politics and administration be kept separate.

The viewpoint that governments can and should be run like a business, free of the irrational and disruptive influences of politics, has never been completely displaced in debates over public management. It continues to be a prominent theme in the rhetoric, though not always the practice, of senior government officials, both elected and appointed. Calls for more businesslike government are regularly heard from chambers of commerce and the editorial pages of newspapers. Royal commissions and task forces established to transform the public sector usually draw much of their inspiration from what appears to work in the private sector.

Of course, there has always been dissent from the generic model. At the risk of considerable oversimplification, three lines of disagreement with the dominant paradigm have emerged over time.

First, critics insisted that the proposal to keep politics separate from administration was naïve, untenable and even undesirable. By reason of the scope and complexity of the public sector, permanent officials, who possessed specialized knowledge, were obliged to play a central role in both the formulation and the implementation of public policy. Not only would politicians rely on them for policy advice, of equal importance public servants were granted wide discretion to refine and to carry out the usually broad, nebulous and multiple goals of legislation by translating them into concrete programs, services and activities.

Second, there was a concerted attack on the earlier notion that a simple set of structural principles and procedural steps could serve as a guaranteed basis for efficient and effective performance. Various critics claimed to have made "intellectual mincemeat" out of earlier, simplified approaches like scientific management and the "principles school," with its snappy acronyms to describe the essential tasks of management. Organizational reality and human motivations were said to be more complicated than the early models of organization life implied

Third, as the field of public administration matured (in part by drawing on empirical social sciences like economics, psychology and sociology), it became more obvious that public bureaucracies were complicated, diverse and dynamic entities with their own identities, cultures, climates and norms of behaviour. The factors motivating people were more numerous and complex than previous theorists had presumed, and the influence of leaders on followers within organizations was mediated by a rich network of groups and influences. There also emerged the concern that bureaucracies had become too powerful, and there was a danger that they would pursue their own narrow self-interest at the expense of the broader public interest defined through the political process and/or the concerns of those groups and individuals on the receiving end of programs.

These challenges to the generic management model reached their peak in the "new public administration" school of 1970s. New public administration (NPA) was a melange of ideas and values rather than a coherent agenda for reform to the public sector. However, "NPAers" could at least agree that public administration, as a field of study and of practice, had to become more relevant to the real problems of society, had to become more humane and less technocratic, and had to bring issues of social equity to the forefront of its concerns. For a decade or two, NPA ideas were a force to be reckoned with in debates over the future of the field. According to George Frederickson, NPA paved the way for the emergence of the new public management and reinventing government movements that gained prominence during the 1990s.[4]

Whereas NPA's influence was subtle and gradual, NPM has been promoted aggressively, with almost evangelical fervour. It offers inspirational stories of apparent successes and the promise of even bigger improvements to come. Lists of irrefutable principles and "dos and don'ts" for creative public managers are prominent. While claiming to be original, many of the organizational and managerial ideas of the NPM school can be traced back to earlier debates in public administration, especially to some of the debates of the 1960s over new public administration.

There are also ways the NPM differs from NPA. First, NPM reflects and reinforces the current suspicion of politics and political institutions. It celebrates and promotes the role of creative and entrepreneurial public servants who are able to avoid or overcome the "constraints" of politics. The implications of this orientation for democracy have not been addressed sufficiently. Secondly, NPM emphasizes the use of markets and competition, reliance on the private sector to deliver public programs, the use of incentives to alter behaviour in public bureaucracies and the adoption of the "best practices" of private firms, such as planning, decentralization, cultural change, results management and putting the customer first. By contrast, the NPA of the 1960s and 1970s was far more concerned with social equity, more humane and democratic administration and with active citizenship as opposed to relatively passive consumerism in the public sector.

By accepting so completely the NPM model, governments have returned to efficiency as the central value of public administration. Facing large deficits earlier and with a legacy of accumulated debt, this emphasis on efficiency is not surprising. In the short run, the new model has brought some increased efficiency and improved services. There are, however, the longer-term implications for governance, particularly for political democracy and the future role of the public service, which have not been fully identified and resolved. The wholesale importation of private management ideas, language and practices into the public sector and the simultaneous export of previously public functions to private entities is changing in a fundamental way the nature of governance in contemporary societies.

Shifts in organizational theory and the recent embrace of NPM ideas by governments has created confusion about the adjective "public" in public administration. At least three definitions of "publicness," as opposed to "privateness," exist today. First, there is the traditional approach that equates public with the institutions of government. Second, there is a broader definition, arising out of the NPA movement, that labels public any activities, whether performed by governmental or non-governmental actors, that are imbued with "the public interest." Activities are deemed to be in the public interest, not on the basis of who authorizes them, but rather on the scope and nature of their impacts on society and its component parts.

A third option is to define "public" in terms of a set of organizational attributes that appear to set governmental organizations apart from their private-sector counterparts. As part of political debate and popular commentary, unflattering comparisons were often made, with the result that a largely negative stereotype of public organizations emerged. However, more objective, empirical research revealed the complications involved with managing publicly: complex and turbulent external and internal environments, multiple, nebulous, shifting and controversial goals, more complicated internal structures and slower decision-making processes, and an absence of straightforward and widely accepted measures of success.[5] Taking into account the distinctive tasks assigned to public organizations and the constraints under which they operate, more balanced assessments of their performance confirmed they were not consistently less efficient or effective than private firms. The same studies also concluded that the differences between public and private organizations were often exaggerated.

Finally, trends within the public sector have produced more hybrids or mixed public–private undertakings, such as private organizations delivering public services, public–private partnerships, and partially privatized public corporations operating in competitive environments. In other words, the organizational world can no longer, if it ever could, be divided neatly into two distinct groups of organizations. As a result of these trends, public managers manage less within integrated organizations and more in collaboration with other organizations, such as other orders of government, private for-profit firms and non-profit organizations. This pattern will require them to develop a somewhat different mix of knowledge and skills in order to manage effectively.

In light of the management writings over the decades and recent trends in the public sector, I conclude that management is more a particularistic than a universal activity that can be conducted according to a formula. However, this perspective presents difficulties in terms of both formulating valid generalizations and offering appropriate advice to managers on how best to perform their jobs. If a more contingent approach to the definition of management fits better with the realities of organizational life, we then must decide which contingencies or factors shape most significantly the management process. In my view, based heavily upon James Q. Wilson's impressive book *Bureaucracy*, task is the single-most important variable, which influences to a considerable, not easily measured extent, such other features of organizational life as the nature of the external and internal environments, the type of people who work in the organization, the nature and content of the issues on its agenda, the culture and climate of the organization, the internal and external patterns of communication, and the distribution of authority and power throughout the organization.[6] Wilson identifies four broad categories of task organizations – production, procedural, craft and coping. David Osborne and Peter Plastrik identify four types of public organizations: policy, regulatory, service and compliance.[7] We need more research and discussion of typologies of different public organizations and their distinctive management processes. My main point is the need to take task seriously in the analysis of the management challenge.

THE MINTZBERG MODEL

If "task" becomes a central explanatory variable, the public-versus-private distinction that has fuelled so much debate in the public administration literature declines in importance, because organizations performing the same task would be expected to confront similar, though not identical, management challenges and would adopt similar approaches. However, in case of public-sector organizations, management is often connected to tasks for which there is no counterpart in the private sector. Professor Mintzberg recognized the distinctive tasks assigned to government in an earlier article.[8] He opens the first chapter in this book by writing that "Managing may be managing, but the public sector is not the private sector." Any managerial model, he continues, must take account of the differences between the two sectors and push harder to incorporate the concept of task as a key variable that shapes his concept of the "frame of the job."

Professor Mintzberg's observations of and interviews with public managers was intended to test and to refine a model of managerial work presented in an earlier article titled "Rounding out the manager's job."[9] My remaining comments will focus on the key concepts that comprise the model and on the methods used to gather information about the nature of management in the public sector. I will have little to say about the rich, nuanced and sometimes vivid interpretations of what he saw and heard about life as a public manager at different levels in different organizations.

The Mintzberg model starts with the individual manager who brings values and style to the job based on his or her experiences, knowledge, competences and mental models. By emphasizing the individual, Mintzberg challenges the universalistic tradition of organizational theory that flows all the way from Frederick Taylor's "one-best-way" of scientific management early in the last century through to more humanistic models like Douglas McGregor's Theory X versus Theory Y.[10] Putting the individual and his or her motivations and perceptions at the centre of organizational theory poses enormous conceptual and analytical challenges.

The nature and development of personal identities is an exceptionally complicated and hence contentious topic among social scientists from various disciplines. As a practical matter, recognizing individual identities as a factor that shapes what management consists of and how managers work through other people poses enormous problems for the development of valid generalizations or even tendency statements. In turn, this creates a barrier to the formulation of reliable prescriptions about how to improve the management process beyond the rather vague advice to take account of the relevant differences among individuals. Robert G. Eccles and Nitin Nohria investigate the problems involved more fully than is possible here.[11]

Placing individuals into a particular organizational context leads them to develop what Mintzberg calls a "job frame." The frame of a job includes "the *purpose* of the job, a particular *perspective* on what needs to be done and specific strategic *positions* for doing it." Someone reading "Managing Publicly" would have difficulty determining the operational meaning of the concepts of purpose, perspective and positions. Mintzberg did a better job clarifying these terms in his article in *Sloan Management Review.*[12]

Mintzberg suggests that job frames can be imposed or invented and can be vague or sharp, and this leads to a four-cell diagram of different "styles" of conceiving the job frame. It is an interesting question whether leadership and management are seen as synonymous in the Mintzberg model. Later in the paper he distinguishes three types of actors: "administrators," who work through information; "leaders," who work through people; and "doers," who prefer direct action. It is not clear which of these actors is most vital to organizational success, presuming that organizations need all three types.

The rhetoric of recent public-service reform initiatives has emphasized the need for public managers to develop stronger leadership skills. The image of the job of public servant has shifted from "administration" (1920s to 1960s) to "management" (1970s to 1980s) to "leadership" (1990s onward). There is likely to be a strong connection between the role perceptions and the job descriptions volunteered by public servants and the ideas about public management that are dominant during a particular period. Evidence of this can be seen in the way that contemporary public servants have embraced so completely, and often uncritically, the ideas of NPM.

Another question that arises is whether public managers are more likely than their private-sector counterparts to have job frames imposed from outside in the form of the statutory mandates of departments, central policy and administrative directives, and system-wide procedural requirements. One suspects that public managers are less free than private managers to invent the parameters of their jobs.

Part of the frame of any job will be the reality and the perceptions of the constraints under which management processes operate. It would be interesting to know the extent to which the constraints are objective and externally imposed versus subjective and internally imposed. To put the issue more concretely, are some people more predisposed than others to act and less likely to perceive constraints on doing so? If governments follow through on their rhetoric about removing or reducing central-agency controls and increasing the autonomy of public managers, will all departments become more innovative, or will some remain reactive because their leadership perceives personal limitations and the constraints imposed by their particular situation?

Surrounding the core of the job is the context defined as three areas – inside, within and outside. These domains are described reasonably precisely, but in practice I wonder whether public managers see reality in more seamless terms than the labels suggest because of the greater interdependence of action and the greater openness to outside influences, characteristic of the public sector compared to the private sector. Reading Mintzberg's accounts of the life of public managers, one gains a sense of the pervasive influence of "politics" of various kinds on the management processes. By politics I mean conflicts among values and among competing interests within organizations. This is a dimension of organizational life that NPM downplays by its emphasis on shared cultures and harmonious relationships. Many forms of politics can arise; for example, conflicts over policy, jurisdiction and status within organizations. A perennial complaint from many public servants concerns the "constraints" on rational management arising from such politics.

Context is further defined in terms of three concentric circles that represent three levels through which managerial work takes place. Mintzberg calls these levels information, people and action. These labels are very close to Eccles and Nohria's description of the essentials of management as rhetoric, people and action.[13] Their perspective emphasizes the initiating role of leaders in terms of communicating a positive vision of the future of the organization. Since he has written about the importance of the symbolic dimensions of the executive's job elsewhere, Mintzberg clearly recognizes the need for leaders to provide meaning and a sense of direction amidst the ambiguity, complexity and uncertainty that characterizes many organizations today.[14]

The communication function of management is emphasized in this paper, but listening is seen as more prevalent than talking. This finding may reflect the organizational levels at which Mintzberg focused his observations. In an ambitious synthesis of the leadership literature, James G. Hunt developed an analytical model that focused on the critical activities of leaders at different organizational levels and on the individual capabilities to fulfil those tasks.[15]

The concept of control has always been central to management thought, but Mintzberg is right to emphasize the multiple meanings and approaches in applying the concept. Eccles and Nohria follow tradition by placing control at the centre of their management model,[16] whereas Mintzberg puts conception of the job frame and communication at the core of his model. Control occupies a less prominent position in his model. It may be that Mintzberg is operating with a more nuanced conception of control.

Under the influence of NPM, governments have increased their use of alternative service-delivery mechanisms. The de-coupling of policy from operations has made the issues related to direction control and accountability more problematic. Increasingly, public management involves the indirect exercise of control through normative means (i.e., the promotion of shared goals and values) rather than the traditional command-and-control procedures of the past. Also, more often than in the past, control is being exercised across organizational boundaries because the public sector has come to rely more on independent or semi-independent parties to deliver programs and services. Other studies tell us that the conduct of external relations with other actors and institutions, both inside and outside of government, are a bigger part of the job of the public manager than that of the manager in a private firm.

It is difficult to comment on the descriptions and analysis of a day-in-the-life of the public managers whom Professor Mintzberg visited and interviewed. The accounts were vivid and has a ring of authenticity to them. The model of the edges was a particularly intriguing notion. The suggestion that individual public servants mainly manage either on the operational, the stakeholder or the political edge suggests that distinctive types of knowledge and skills are required to be successful at different levels in public organizations – a point that Mintzberg raises in his rather abbreviated conclusion. I would have liked to have seen this analysis pushed further. For one thing, the analysis reveals the artificiality of the "steering-versus-rowing" distinction behind the reinventing government movement. Reading the descriptions of managerial life, one appreciates that policy ("steering") and operations ("rowing") are actually points along a continuum and that a strict organizational separation of the two activities could potentially impair learning at both the individual and the organizational level. Also, a more dynamic model that captures the actual interactive process reveals the interdependencies among ideas and decision-making at different levels and across organizations.

CONCLUSION

The Mintzberg paper provides us with a rich and nuanced description of the real world of public managers. Social scientists have criticized the management gurus for relying on stories told to them by corporate executives as evidence on which to base glib prescriptions for organizational success. Storytelling is not irrelevant, however. What managers convey through stories is their definition of reality. However, it is a better research method to go beyond reporting on the anecdotes of managers to observe their actual behaviour and then integrate their words and actions into a theoretical model. Mintzberg is attempting to do this, and he should be praised for his efforts. If the concepts are not entirely clear, it is because the phenomenon under study defies simple specification and precise measurement. The world of management is complex. If we are to write about that world in all its complexity, we will need to invent concepts that accurately represent reality but that are also presented in language that is understandable and resonates with people outside of the academic community. Scholars of public management also contribute to the definition of reality. Those scholars like Professor Mintzberg who use language and metaphors that public servants find most evocative of their managerial world will be more successful in having their ideas influence public management practice.

NOTES

1 Michael M. Harmon and Richard T. Mayer, *Organization Theory for Public Administration* (Toronto: Little Brown and Company, 1986), p. 61.
2 Robert Behn, "Management by groping along," *Journal of Policy Analysis and Management* 7, no. 4 (Fall 1988), pp. 643–63.
3 Henry Mintzberg, "Managing government, governing management," *Harvard Business Review* 74, no. 3 (May/June 1996), pp. 75–83.
4 H. George Frederickson, *The Spirit of Public Administration* (San Francisco: Jossey-Bass, 1997).
5 Hal G. Rainey, *Understanding and Managing Public Organizations*, 2nd edition (San Francisco: Jossey-Bass, 1997).
6 James Q. Wilson, *Bureaucracy: What government agencies do and why they do it* (New York: Basic Books, 1989).
7 David Osborne and Peter Plastrik, *Banishing Bureaucracy: The Five Strategies for Reinventing Government* (Reading, Mass.: Addison-Wesley, 1997).
8 Mintzberg, "Managing government, governing management," *Harvard Business Review.*
9 Henry Mintzberg, "Rounding out the manager's job," *Sloan Management Review* 36, no. 1 (Fall 1994), pp. 11–26.
10 Frederick W.Taylor, *The Principles of Scientific Management* (New York: Harper, 1911); Douglas McGregor, *The Human Side of Enterprise* (New York: McGraw-Hill, 1960).
11 Robert G. Eccles and Nitin Nohria, *Beyond the Hype: Rediscovering the Essence of Management* (Boston: Harvard Business School Press, 1992).
12 Mintzberg, "Rounding out the manager's job," *Sloan Management Review.*
13 Eccles and Nohria, *Beyond the Hype*, Part I.
14 Frances Westley and Henry Mintzberg, "Visionary leadership and strategic management," *Strategic Management Journal* 10 (Summer 1989), pp. 17–32.
15 James G. Hunt, *Leadership: a New Synthesis* (Newbury Park, Calif.: Sage Publications, 1991).
16 Eccles and Nohria, *Beyond the Hype.*

9

The Mintzberg Model and Some Empirical Evidence: Putting it to the Test[1]

Jacques Bourgault

In this chapter I want to verify and illustrate Henry Mintzberg's general explicative model with three empirical tests I undertook recently in the Canadian federal public sector. In 1993, I concluded a study of federal deputy ministers' time management, when Henry Mintzberg was doing his own interviews. With a second study, I, along with Stéphane Dion, in 1994, examined government ministers' satisfaction with the public managerial roles performed by deputy ministers between 1984 and 1993. The third study involved a series of semi-structured interviews with "senior management specialists" that I concluded at the end of 1998, along with Donald Savoie. The purpose of the research was to study the perspectives for the evolution of the roles of senior public managers. Our comments here deal mostly with deputy ministers of all the federal departments, while the preceding chapters by Professor Mintzberg have dealt with all levels of managers and only three departments; those variations may explain some of the differences in the observations I make.

The administrators who, as professionals and technicians, apply policies and programs to cases they receive, are not dealt with in this chapter, because Mintzberg's model cannot address them without my having to introduce important nuances throughout the discussion. We shall, therefore, deal mostly with managers at various senior and intermediate levels who make sure that what must be done gets done. It should be noted, however, that Mintzberg's remarks do not apply equally to all the managers discussed in this chapter.

Mintzberg's sample does not pretend to be representative, for there are far too few respondents by level or by organization. On the other hand, his study makes possible a longitudinal reading of public organizations in three different sites (Parks, the RCMP and Justice), in three different regions of Canada. Mintzberg develops rich observations through his vast analytical, research and publishing experience in the area of senior management in organizations. In this chapter, we shall verify and, as need be, comment on the proposed explicative model, relying on the observations from the three empirical studies mentioned above.

JOB FRAME

The job frame elaborated by Mintzberg (objectives of the position, organizational diagnosis, strategies to do what should be done) comes from personal qualifications that people bring with them to the workplace (e.g., values, experiences, models, knowledge, skills). The heart of managerial work, then, focuses on the relations between the unit managed, the rest of the organization and its environment. The senior manager must conceive this job frame (what is to be done) and then program the necessary action to do it. This conceptual and programmatic space depends on the hierarchical level of the position (varying greatly from deputy minister to the directors, all the way to the team leader, passing through four to six other levels of managers and administrators).

The Conception and Programming of the Job Frame

The way one approaches one's work comes from two sources – personal predispositions and the mandate – the latter of which, in the public sector, generally comes from outside the position or the administrative unit.

I offer four observations about "predispositions" for the managerial levels in public management:

First, descending the organizational hierarchy, one finds oneself more likely in the zone of interpreting the mandate rather than conceptualizing it, as the zone of intellectual autonomy is more restricted. The obligation to reinforce the pressure of the mandate is greater in the position of middle management than in that of senior management.

Second, the more one finds oneself in a legally constrained situation near the centre of the organizational mandate, the more the "open" zone of conceptualization diminishes. This holds particularly true in the public sector, where the courts deliver a restricted interpretation of the mandate. A good understanding of the legal framework of the work is critical in the public sector, particularly at the senior levels where the operational benchmarks (Standard Operational Procedures) are rarer.

Third, public organizations have historically situated their action in the camp of legal conformity, rather than seizing opportunities, because the model of action in the public sector is, first of all, to apply the law to its full extent. It would be considered an inexcusable bureaucratic abuse (anti-democratic and illegal) if an organization or a manager neglected his or her legal duty in order to "seize an opportunity" or to "personally reconceptualize the application of a piece of legislation." This observation leads us to consider that in general, this window of opportunity enlarges as one goes from the departments and the quasi-judicial bodies to the state-owned businesses. There are, however, within the departments certain zones more amenable to conceptualization than others (planning and communication versus operations).

Fourth, new public management (NPM) calls upon this traditional rule of favouring legal conformity, as the interviews of autumn 1998 have shown. One anticipates a new form of "government according to the provider model" (the organizer and provider, rather than the achiever), where the direct operational activities are reduced to a minimum and carried out by autonomous governmental agencies linked together by only a few common legitimizing principles. Managers are now required to manage by results rather than by activity and to worry about the final outcome, not just legalities. They are required to act in a framework of greater decentralization and empowerment. They are forced to associate with partners in the non-profit private sector who do not have the same legal constraints. Finally, they must interact more with public bodies, politicians and pressure groups, which increases the pressure for transparency, sometimes even creating moral contradictions for them. Should they serve the law in its rigidity or try to find ways of applying it to meet the demands of these milieus? While such innovations seem attractive in the short run, they could have adverse effects in the long term.

There is no precise job description for deputy ministers. It is a variable, multifaceted job, depending on political schedules, political crises and events arising from both outside and inside the organization. Interpretation of the government will play a predominant role in the conception of their job frame.[2] In everyday life, the deputy ministers in the 1993 study protected themselves with blocks of uninterrupted work time in order to think about their priorities or "do long-term planning," alone or with their staff. They devoted about twenty per cent of their time to this endeavour, and some would go into work on the weekends to make use of quality thinking time.

Certain specialists interviewed in 1998 fear the conceptual reductionism that flows from the strong homogeneous federal recruitment at the senior level: the Russian doll syndrome. They are of the opinion that the diversity of social problems calls for a greater diversity of recruitment.

Passing on the Mandate

A second factor produces the manager's "job frame," namely, the mandate confided to him or her by the outside environment. This mandate is not limited only to the "what" of work, but also to the diverse "how" of this same work, that is, the relationships in the milieu and with employees, the degree of involvement in the job, the initiative, and fighting spirit expected.

Public managers get signals concerning the expected mandate at the time of their nomination, when they take up the position and during the annual cycle of corporate management planning. Each deputy minister or CEO of a government organism knows very well that he or she was chosen within a precise context, by people (politicians and senior civil servants) with certain expectations, and for certain reasons, which all too often have to do with particular skills, specific characteristics or past achievements. Many series of interviews we conducted with ministers and deputy ministers showed that they saw themselves with a mandate of policy development, policy consolidation or organizational development. During the informal selection process, the interviews dealt mostly with the specific organizational diagnostic, with the conceptualization of the mandate, and the work style. This work style concerns how the roles are assumed, a topic I shall discuss below.

Once nominated, the deputy ministers and directors of agencies meet the clerk and secretary of the Privy Council Office (PCO), the most senior civil servant, to discuss the "terms of the mandate." They also meet the minister to learn "his agenda and priorities." Federal deputy ministers internalize both a sectoral and a corporative vision of the mandate through a group socialization process. One slowly "becomes" a deputy minister, and one's colleagues have input into one's career development, as well as one's performance evaluation and its financial and professional consequences. The frequent and in-depth group discussions (weekly lunches, COSO, CCMD, closed retreats every three months, etc.) contribute to developing a sectoral mandate that is followed by every federal senior civil servant.

The mandate is communicated to senior management by various means. These include the perception of expectations during the selection process; the definition of performance objectives with one's superior; finalizing work plans (annual or for several years, the business plan, etc); and, above all, the operation of the management committees of the organization (e.g., planning committees, work groups). Finally, the bilateral management meetings serve to circulate and control the mandate.

Two means of communication serve to disseminate the manager's perception of the mandate: directed communication and the organizational culture. The first transmits the visions of the mandate by the policies, programs, norms, directives and supervision. Meanwhile, the organizational culture, the product of past organizational legends, takes on a diffuse latent form and is reinforced by statements of mission/mandate/values or by operations such as "total quality," etc.

Programming Operations

At the top of public organizations, programming activities have to take place in a framework of very particular constraints, where the deputy minister works under the direction of the minister, who is a politician, most likely elected, responsible before Parliament and the population. Programming is particularly subject to sensitivities and political agendas, coloured by the values and struggles of the day, which often limit ambitions, means, creativity and efficiency. With all due respect for democracy, public managers deal very well with the constraints, as the studies of ministers' satisfaction with their deputy ministers show. In particular, the ministers praised the loyalty of their deputy ministers, their respect for authority, their role as "political radar" as well as their performance during parliamentary commissions. The deputy ministers' roles concerning political sensitivity seem as much, if not more, appreciated by the ministers than the managerial roles they also play!

Additionally, when they direct their attention inside the organization and towards corresponding groups in civil society, deputy ministers benefit from a large range of intervention strategies for which they enjoy uncontested powers. This holds true as long as they stay in the political corridor set out by the minister, within the budgetary framework and respect the standard governmental process. As general administrator and principal non-partisan adviser to the minister in political matters, deputy ministers have important authority and powers at their disposal, permitting them unique resources for action.

The 1993 federal deputy ministers placed primary importance on programming in their schedule. They set their more than sixty-hour-week schedule according to the amount of time they decided to devote to prioritized items and to preferred types of intervention. "You must only do those things that you can do by yourself and that have the greatest repercussions on your game plan."[3] Mintzberg's cases of John Tait and Norman Inkster demonstrate well this approach to the job frame.

The senior manager or regional director, more protected from the interventions of politicians and the public than is the minister, program their time allocations, such that they find themselves more inwardly directed in the organization, communicating with a more restricted range of stakeholders from the civil society. These managers will find that conforming to the corporative agenda of the minister (endorsed by the deputy minister), as well as the conviviality of the interventions of the minister's colleagues, plus the interventions of the central agencies and other public bodies acting in the same domain, put particular limits on their actions.

MANAGING BY INFORMATION: COMMUNICATING, CONTROLLING

For Mintzberg, the family of roles closest to the central core of the managers' job is that which concerns information. If the definition of the job frame makes managers decide what should be done, the appropriate action on information will make them "do such that ... (it) will be done." In this model, information implies both communication and control.

Communication, which involves obtaining and diffusing information, occupied forty per cent of managers' time, which would make senior managers both the internal and external nerve centre of the organization, inasmuch as, given their privileged relationships, they possess and share exclusive non-verbal and unwritten information.

Our interviews with deputy ministers concerning their time management reveal that, twenty years after the first of Mintzberg's studies on CEOs, deputy ministers spend even more time than before collecting and diffusing information. They seem to spend most of their time in various meetings in order to fulfil this role of nerve centre or "market place" of numerous organizational subsystems – the minister, the department, the management team, colleagues, clients. As external spokespersons, they intervene in inter-ministerial committees, federal–provincial committees, congresses and conferences with groups connected to the department, etc.[4] As internal circulators, they transmit orientations and plans of the government and the senior management team of senior civil servants during management committees. They visit regional offices and organize discussion days with all the employees. The study we conducted in 1993 of almost all the deputy ministers showed that they spent only five per cent of their time with their minister, ten per cent with colleagues, forty per cent with their assistants, and forty per cent with the external environment.[5] Finally, they spent five per cent of their time alone, working in their office.

We should not minimize the double dimension of their roles. Deputy ministers are the departmental figureheads for the external environment, as well as figureheads for the government (in the sense of a corporative structure) with respect to departmental employees. On the other hand, as the communicator, they also address the outside to increase the awareness of these environments to the orientations, projects and preoccupations of ministerial services.

Lower down the hierarchy, middle managers act as figureheads much more fortuitously. If this is sometimes the case for regional directors with respect to their milieus, or for certain general managers vis-à-vis specialized pressure groups, it is not so for other managers. Rare are those who brandish their governmental spokesperson role outside the bureaus.

Control refers to the selective use of information to orient subordinates' action by setting up systems, modifying structures and establishing directives. This orientation or guidance function permits the management task to shift from information roles to people roles.

Deputy ministers enjoy few exclusive powers, but they have the use of many powers delegated by the central agencies and the minister, such as the power to make decisions about managing resources, policies and programs. They can partly delegate most of their powers to their senior managers and intermediaries, and, as one descends the hierarchy, the extent of the delegated decisions is limited. The modification of structures entails the assignment of personnel, and the issuing of directives deals mostly with micro-work processes.

The 1993 interviews showed the importance deputy ministers give to the implementation and fine-tuning of management systems as instruments of control: "It's better to adopt a system that works, than to have to find solutions in the middle of a crisis!" In 1995, the conservative ministers were satisfied with eighty-one per cent of the minister/deputy minister teams. Management of the department, however, ranked among the five lowest of the eighteen components rated. The ministers had the impression that, during the period from 1984 and 1993, the deputy ministers showed minimal interest in systems, resource or operations management.[6]

The systems, structures and directives that frame administrative action come largely from outside the department. The central agencies, the departments with a horizontal function, and the principles of administrative law also become vital for the managers, limiting their room to manœuvre. External constraints are more numerous and restrictive in the public sector than in the private sector. The movement to create relatively autonomous agencies, which is an expression of NPM, would leave managers more operational leeway, thus increasing the magnitude of the subordinates' control role. Subordinates are less restricted, but they have to be "oriented" by control.

MANAGING THROUGH PEOPLE: DIRECTING, LINKING

In his model, Mintzberg explains that managers should motivate their people, empower them, influence them and make them get involved. The leadership and liaison roles permit managers to follow through with these activities.

As leader, managers generate and disseminate the energy and the soul of the organization; they practise bilateral management with each of their subordinates. They will create, manage and lead teams, and provide organizational leadership, thus orienting and reinforcing the organizational culture (for example, by playing the "figurehead" role during symbolic activities).

In 1993, the deputy ministers supervised, on average, fifteen immediate subordinates. They exercised their leadership mainly in strategic management operations (e.g., plans, mission-mandate statements) at internal management and directors' committee meetings, during official ceremonies of awards and inaugurations, at conferences organized periodically for the employees and managers, and during visits to each of the regions. Half of the deputy ministers in 1993 chose the committee meeting as the management tool of choice, followed by twenty-five per cent who opted for direct supervision during management meetings. Few deputy ministers chose either supervision by results (at a distance) or the open-door policy.[7]

The respondents of 1998 were unanimous in acknowledging the need for leadership as one of the three absolute priorities in tomorrow's manager's profile. The leader is expected to treat his or her people like persons ("Let's move to the soft stock"), to practise a leadership that listens, and to manage and motivate first by the culture. This reinforces Mintzberg's observations for RCMP and requires the managing through culture that he favours.

In the public sector, the performance of these roles has not always been as important as we seem to think. Practising their legal authority can distract directors from their interest in adequately stimulating the "affect" of the employees towards the organization and its mission or towards themselves as director. Moreover, employee tenure and statutory remuneration can render them more impermeable to the punctual stimuli generated by the leader. Furthermore, in the past, focusing the public organization on implementing legislation (regardless of cost or consequence) limited the manager's role as external link to the other governmental milieus (e.g., the corresponding departments, central agencies) and hindered any exterior influence from endangering the "correct application of the law."

More precisely, the recent interviews have showed that the new public managers should invest in the people who work with them. The respondents believed that the system of public management should consider people as individuals with a right to their uniqueness, who need to contribute their utmost to the organization, and not just as numbers in the system. Thanks to technology, public organizations will require, more and more, a workforce at the professional and managerial levels. Increasingly, their creativity and sensitivity will be called upon, and managers must create the conditions for the optimal development of human resources. Here we are describing a listening leadership, which is not really accommodated in Mintzberg's model. The employees' perception that the listening is sincere, attentive and profound provides a leadership of proximity, where the leader's decisions and attitudes are closer to the expectations of the employees the manager is trying to mobilize.

The study of Canadian deputy ministers' time management in 1993 fully confirms the importance of these leadership roles (subordinate direction, team direction, organizational leadership) and of the liaison roles. In 1993, a deputy minister would participate, on average, in five ministerial committees and twelve formal committees of the governmental corporation – signs of increasing horizontal management.[8] In the case of a department dealing with clients and provincial relations, deputy ministers take part in up to ten extra-governmental committees. These weekly or half-yearly corporate meetings are critical opportunities to pass on information, where the deputy minister plays a pivotal role in the preparation of the agenda, analysis of preparatory documents, discussion of positions to defend, debriefings, follow-up to decisions, setting up technical subcommittees.[9] In 1993, they criticized the excessive number of committees and the time required for each one of them. Doubting the usefulness of these meetings, the deputy ministers complained that they were not well prepared, nor well run. Did these deputy ministers really accept this dimension of their role, or were they protesting against the little time that was left after they played their relational role? Is such a disproportionate demand on time inevitable in a large and complex public service that recognizes the right of innumerable actors to intervene?[10]

The conservative ministers, commenting in 1995 on their 103 deputy ministers' performance of the eighteen aspects of their role, gave them a satisfactory grade: eighty-one per cent of the minister/deputy minister teams were judged satisfactory over all. The item "influence in the bureaucracy" received the lowest performance grade, with twenty-nine per cent of the minister/deputy minister teams being judged unsatisfactory. These numbers say much more about the ministers' high expectations than of the real influence of the deputy ministers on their colleagues. On another relational dimension, eighteen per cent of the teams were considered unsatisfactory. The dimension in question concerned the deputy ministers' ability to persuade the department's pressure groups and clients. These statistics are comparable to those of a former Quebec study on the same topic.

As liaison officer, deputy ministers represent their organization on the outside by creating networks and coalitions to better satisfy organizational needs, defending the organization and bringing back favourable information, resources and decisions. Deputy ministers also bring back information and influence that originated in the environment. They must then judiciously regulate the delivery of this information and influence in order to protect the organization from exaggerated and disorganized influence and also to keep the organization from turning inward, thus depriving it of influence and contact with the exterior reality. Deputy ministers appear to be the nerve centre of the system, the entry point for information, and the disseminator of this information from the organization. Sometimes their double allegiance as deputy minister to the minister and member of the government's group of deputy ministers creates a "cronelian" dilemma.[11] If they select an information strategy favourable to the governmental corporation, they risk being seen as a weak leader by their employees. Their "job frame" dictates that they have to do a balancing act.

The public manager of the future, if one is to believe the practitioners queried in 1998, should develop and maintain an optimal network of relations with officials in all circles ("You are worth your on-line network with civil society."). He or she should find the appropriate means to create a continuous dialogue with civil society (the "citizen's engagement" trend) and take up the challenge of improving the image of public management and the state presented in the media. Public management by partnership forces public managers to be proactive in creating such partnerships, thereby keeping well informed of possible opportunities available at other government levels and/or in civil society.

MANAGING BY ACTION: DOING, NEGOTIATING

Mintzberg describes two sets of action roles for managers: "doing" and "negotiating." In the first case, even though managers should delegate tasks rather than do them themselves, one often sees them taking the "bull by the horns." They will then personally promote a project, personally deal with crises and emergencies, personally "deliver" the diagnoses of problems and their solutions, make decisions official, or, in the end, initiate changes in their organization. Occasionally they will do the work of one of their employees, or they may continue to carry out certain of their former tasks.

The deputy ministers spent sixteen per cent of their time dealing with crises and answering emergencies. They told us that they spend twenty per cent of their time on strategic files that will move forward or change their organization. None of them, however, admitted to spending time on tasks from their former jobs or on the tasks normally done by their employees.[12] To champion a file in the public domain does not so much imply "doing" it as it does to officially support it, personalize it and make it a flagship. In the 1998 interviews, the dimension of "doing" appeared to be reduced to a strict minimum, leaving all the time and energy for conception, liaison, getting things done, and negotiation. Doing too much oneself is the archetype of the bad manager, whose "systems don't work." "Make sure that you have the right people to make your plans work," say the deputy ministers.[13]

Deputy ministers negotiate agreements with partners, conduct negotiations after concluding agreements, and negotiate during critical moments in the evolution of important organizational files. During the 1993 interviews, the subject of negotiations did not actually come up in the discussions, probably because it is omnipresent and obvious in an implicit form. Every meeting, every encounter, every document expressing positions is a form of negotiation: negotiation is a continual process of interpersonal relations.

Today, the context has changed and negotiations have taken a much more formalistic turn. In the 1998 study, many senior civil servants predicted that formal negotiations, as much with the external environment as inside the government machine, would constitute one of the principal occupations of public managers of tomorrow. Their partnerships, their contracting-out, and their mandates delegated to other bodies will keep them continually negotiating agreements and ways of enforcing them. As a corollary, they will devote a large part of their time negotiating manœuvring room for themselves with the central agencies and the horizontal ministries or "selling" the validity of these agreements to the authorities. They will look for "quick fixers" and "sound risk-takers" who are capable of negotiating agreements that can be "appreciated in terms of results and impact rather than in the usual vague terms," they told us.

MANAGEMENT STYLES

The challenges of each position and each personality, as well as the different contexts of management influence the manager's role selection. Some managers will adopt a more "conceptual" style, others will take on an "administrative" style, some an "interpersonal relations" style, or the style of the "person of action." The style emerges from the managers' attitudes and how they play their daily role. In the departments, the cerebral deductive approach (a move from the inner to the outer circles of Mintzberg's model) would be favoured. The complexity of societal problems today could justify a "visionary" style for the manager. Mintzberg wants to make this approach more present in the manuals, recruitment and training of managers.

In 1993, the federal deputy ministers favoured by far the conceptual style. The administrative roles that are too weighty go mostly to the assistants. The interpersonal relations style exists but not at the expense of the conception style, while personal activism is frowned upon. The crisis context of public finance and political uncertainty do not encourage the emergence of visionaries who would tend to impose their own views on democratic programming in society. They recognize, however, that everything is changing more and more quickly and that there is a greater need for openness outside the governmental organization.

The 1995 study of conservative ministers who wanted to put their stamp on a policy development agenda showed a very high level of expectation for their deputy ministers. In one of the rare high levels of dissatisfaction found in the study, nineteen per cent of the conservative ministers said they were dissatisfied with the ability of deputy ministers to design policy. A study done in 1990 of ministers in the Parti québécois government in Quebec produced similar results.[14]

The ministers interviewed in 1998, who were well away from the constraints of the daily action, appeared to favour the conception style, the interpersonal relations style and the visionary style, which would fit well with the new realities of state management. This situation includes more complex and more global problems; reality changing more rapidly than ever before; the presence of more but under-utilized technology; problems characterized by interface and horizontality; and the presence of a more informed, demanding and critical public.

Yet none of the 1998 respondents wanted "pure visionaries" as senior managers, so heavy is the burden of the political milieus, pressure groups and central agencies. The contribution "visionary" should "absolutely exist in the federal administration," they believed, "but in a reasonable dose and without losing sight of the necessities of the reality of the power relations we enter into." The vision must be a part of a more global and appropriate integrator style, following a clear reading of the context, and developing out of the "well-rounded manager job."

CONCLUSION

This review of Mintzberg's model links it much more to senior managers (deputy ministers, associates, delegates and assistants, presidents and directors of government bodies) than to middle managers and administrators.

The conception of the job frame seems to be ever-changing and is mostly directed from the outside. Within a limited legal framework, however, managers have a large range of means available to them. Programming the agenda, as defined by Mintzberg, appears crucial and gives a lot of leeway to deputy ministers. They situate their action at the centre of a communication network where they are very active, and they tend to get involved indirectly and subtly (through meetings) in the control activities described by Mintzberg.

The deputy ministers manage through people much more by their networking than by the leadership activity, which seems to be more sporadic and dependent on the personality of each deputy minister. They carry out very little themselves, apart from building relationships, animation and presence at meetings and resolution of isolated crises. Today, their roles as negotiators are much more in demand within the framework of new public management.

The most valued style remains conceptualization, followed by interpersonal relations. In the public sector, the latter could never compensate for the lack of the former. The style of visionary seems to colour the conceptualization in the new societal context of changing complexity, for which the policies are to be conceived and implanted.

The largest part of the model applies to the ministerial public sector. It is possible that a study of the CEOs of state-owned companies would show that they tend to enjoy more autonomy in the execution of the roles found in Mintzberg's model.

NOTES

1 I am grateful to Gladys L. Symons, professor, École nationale d'administration publique, for translating this chapter.

2 Jacques Bourgault, "De Kafka au Net : la lutte de tous les instants pour le contrôle de l'agenda chez les sous-ministres canadiens," *Gestion* 22, no. 2 (June 1997), pp. 21–3.

3 Ibid., pp. 22–3.

4 Ibid., p. 20.

5 Ibid., p. 21.

6 Jacques Bourgault, "The satisfaction of ministers with the performance of their deputy ministers during the Mulroney government: 1984–1993." Research Paper, No. 22, Canadian Centre for Management Development, 1997, p. 23.

7 Bourgault, "De Kafka au Net," *Gestion*, p. 25.

8 Jacques Bourgault, "Horizontal integration at the top," *Optimum* 27, no. 4 (December 1997), p. 22.

9 Bourgault, "De Kafka au Net," *Gestion*, p. 25.

10 Bourgault, "Horizontal integration at the top," *Optimum*, p. 22.
11 Ibid., p. 16.
12 Bourgault, "De Kafka au Net," *Gestion*, p. 22.
13 Ibid.
14 Jacques Bourgault and Stéphane Dion, "La satisfaction des ministres envers leurs hauts fonctionnaires : le cas du gouvernement du Québec, 1976–1985," CANADIAN PUBLIC ADMINISTRATION 33, no. 3 (Fall 1990), pp. 414–37.

Conclusions[1]

Jacques Bourgault

So, where are we now? The first part of this book traced the development of a model based on the conclusions of its author, who has long been interested with private-sector organizations and who based his work on eight "one-day-in-the-life" studies of eight federal managers in three different departments. The second part of this book began with practical comments of some fifteen civil servants in managerial positions who work in a variety of government jurisdictions. Finally, four academics from management, public administration and political science commented on Mintzberg's model from their own perspective, looking at comparative career paths and characteristics, practical aspects of the deputy minister's job, the impact of new public management, and the very essence of public service.

We have seen that each manager's movements involves constant integration of the manager's personal characteristics, the job frame, and agenda-setting; he or she strives to achieve results in leading the unit as well as in relating the unit to its environment. Although the complexity and type of strategy depends on the level at which one is working, all managers must deal primarily with information processing, then with people, and finally with action; in so doing, they perform the specific roles of the eight managers as described in Mintzberg's model.

This integrated approach sheds new light on the manager's role in that each communication, action and decision can no more be seen as separate or sequential. An individual can't just work according to his or her interests or according to what he or she thinks is important or the fad in town, because, rather than being mutually exclusive, these roles complement each other.

Many approaches from administrative science and private management were adopted by the public sector: the POSDCORB approach (planning, organizing, staffing, directing, coordinating, reporting and budgeting);

the classical view of resources management (i.e., organizational design, human and material resources); the impact's level approach of making strategic, tactical and operational decisions; and finally the common environmental approach of managing "up, down, out and in." Mintzberg's model is not a theory, since it does not inform us what attitudes, behaviour, decisions, actions should or will occur given a particular set of conditions. Instead, it tries to explain the "how" and "why" of managers' behaviour. It may lead someday to a more theoretical exposé.

Mintzberg's model serves as an integrated explanation of these various approaches. POSDCORB is based largely on the job frame and focuses on information, people and action; the resource management approach is also relevant to the explanatory model in that it touches on information, people and the negotiation roles (Mintzberg's cases let us see how it varies at different hierarchical managerial levels); the environmental approach also adopts much of the model and touches on communication, liaison and negotiation roles. This model covers and integrates many relatable approaches.

What is apparent from much of this work is that the model needs further analysis about the specifics of each hierarchical level of management, of public and parapublic sectors, and about the impact of new public management (that at times makes the two sectors more alike but that likely also, over painful learning experiences, establishes more fundamental boundaries between both sectors' core components. Huguette Labelle, Ralph Heintzman, Louis Bernard and others have highlighted the similarities and the differences in the private sector's managerial role).

The discussion by Mintzberg and particularly the debate among practitioners have illustrated the growing use of organizational design as a response to facing changing corporate challenges. In looking at organizations such as Parks Canada, RCMP, and the Department of Justice, Mintzberg effectively discussed the virtual network, the doughnut and the hub. The tri-dimensional composition of these organizations is particularly striking, in the sense that in the past relations were considered either vertically on the hierarchical mode or horizontally on the corporate mode. The matrices (RCMP), the ad hoc multilevels and multidepartmental (Justice) contributions to action as well as the cultural flows that contribute continuously to the construction of decisions and actions are taken into account. This involves not only the lower layers of the organizations but also the ongoing "conversation" with civil society as users or benefactors (case of Montreal police) or as the politically influential (in the cases of the City of Montreal and Montreal hospital). In this context, the manager's role, more than ever, is to find, clarify and share an organization's sense of direction, as Diane Wilhelmy and Gérard Divay have rightly noted.

Without exception, everyone judged the "job-frame approach" to be of equal importance to all managers. It was mentioned that in the public sector, "job frame" is very seldom left to the manager's preference: the purposes are made of pre-existing legal or political constraints, and the perspective about the job is the locus of several interactions pulling in different directions between the manager and the environment that he or she selected or that was imposed on him or her; much of the game involves "who is going to select the frame?"; it is more often "driven" than "open"; there appears also to be some *vagueness* to this process, given the very nature of demands for a public good and the specifics of its production and delivery; since the parameters of a public good are not easy to define and since political masters may find appropriate "to occasionally vary their instructions to public-sector managers. Vague plans should be distinguished from ones that are more precise but that are "constantly changing"; the former allows room for manœuvring while the latter is simply the multiplication of inconsistent orders. Authors on bureaucracy and on organizations always described some margin of manœuvre in how a public-sector manager will address an issue, depending on the level of risk he or she is willing to tolerate and how far and how fast this person wants to go.

This also points to the reality of a public-sector paradox, which arises when one considers the numerous and varied personal styles that exist in such a heavily ruled domain. This is probably more so than in the private sector where, even if management should adapt to a firm's clientele, products and milieu, practice is actually dictated by what has been taught at business school or celebrated at the latest discussion on the cocktail circuit. The public sector involves so many different subcultures and different social and political actors that personal style may just be a natural answer to the job's particular challenges.

Dealing with *information*, we have seen how effective communication may be more critical in the public sector than anywhere else; this is due to the number, diversity and power of the competing civil, political and administrative actors who take issue with whatever you do or want to do as a public manager. The controlling function through organizational design exists, although it is less important in the public sector since its organizational design is so rigorous, complex and driven by so many actors. Part of the game is annihilation of the other's efforts to control the specifics of any organizational design. In fact, most of the real rather than formal control business still resides in communication, formal and cultural.

With respect to *people*, the debate made it clear how difficult it is to be a leader: you are always a leader under attack (target of bureaucratic, political, economical and corporate pressures); a leader not easily permitted to be "the champion" of something (anonymity, low profile waiting for success to celebrate); and a leader having to live many different (when not competing) loyalties! As a leader, you can reproduce the culture, protect the organization and personify the authority; when you are allowed to have the political and legal margin of manœuvre you champion some important changes for which you are likely to be equally feared and envied, encouraged and blocked, praised and blamed, depending on interests, timing, changing moods and residual influence with power brokers. It is like this in private sector, except for the consequences of being praised and blamed.

Effective *liaison*, for the reasons previously discussed with communication, is really crucial to the public sector; the model tends to present liaison as more personal and horizontal and communication as more formal and vertical, even though they are not exclusively so. The role of each should be more differentiated in the model.

Action deals mostly with doing and negotiating. "Real" doing is not the practice at the top of the public sector although some doing does exist in tiny proportion – personally calling the clerk, preparing informal notes, or making performance appraisal for immediate subordinates. In turn, negotiating is everywhere and probably more present here where there is a more defined division of power. As Paul Thomas noted, *negotiation* is likely to be even more important, given recent changes in new public management that involves among other things, service-delivery practices involving more partners.

As a representative of an organization's values, a manager's organizational style has an impact on society at large; it is reflected in the environmental scan, the situation, the game plan. How the organization is portrayed to the outside depends on those calls made by the manager. In this way, the public experience is not that different from the upper-level management experience in the private sector.

Much has been said about the adverse effects of *politics* on public management; others would argue that politics affects the public management for democratic and legitimacy purposes. Recall that all three levels at Parks Canada were concerned with politics in terms of traffic management, regional pressures and national policy. It always seems more blatant in the fields where issues are not symbolic but material and where the game is not played according to the subtle code prevailing in any capital.

If politics is commonplace in the public sector, some would argue that it is also quite common in the private sector. Private managers try not to hurt local consumers so as to avoid complaints to regulation boards. They build their game plan having in mind regional considerations for opportunities and by maintaining a positive image. At every organization's level, private managers play power games for budgets, resources, appointments, etc.; at the corporate level, they will try to influence public policy so that government regulations, including controls, contracts, subsidies, tax breaks, are as beneficial as possible.

Although each organization has its share of politics, one difference between both sectors is that outside forces affect to a greater degree the internal politics of the public sector; second, the public sector serves more as a political target (for the private sector, pressure groups and the media); third, the private sector acts more like a political assailant in the system, initiating some of the political games when the public sector is more "reactive" to them. In all sectors, a political manager's behaviour encompasses mutual adjustments, use of symbols, playing against each other's different interests. They all tend to gain autonomy for designing and implementing the job frame, which is political everywhere.

Mintzberg's comments made in his chapter on Parks Canada about plans, procedures, buzzwords, etc., anything that comes from Ottawa seems a bit strong. Of course, it is not hard to believe that field employees think boardroom executives don't always understand grassroot issues; it's probably the case for Gord's employees' attitudes towards him, as well as that of outfitters towards Parks staff and maybe that of elk towards outfitters. If someone thinks regulation for public interest is the problem, think again: some endangered species would have welcomed a timely management plan when their population was not in danger of being eradicated. Individuals in organizations routinely campaign for more autonomy and less control from the centre. Someone thinking we just have to let employees carry on the way they want to "because they are nearer the terrain," is overlooking problems such as narrow concern, productivity and bureaucratic self-interest.

Nonetheless, strategic plans and mission statements may sometimes defy common sense. For example, the University of Quebec once had dozens of general policies that led to hundreds of operational policies, including one on where to store the policies. There was even another policy on how to use emergency exits in case of fire! Policies do help to steer people in the proper course, encouraging them to think about what they should do and how. People tend to criticize paradigms they do not master well, or they tend to minimize the importance or ignore what is new, looks threatening, or what they are not good at. Thus front-line people will say a strategic plan is too immaterial, and head office people will say that field opinions are too narrow, ad hoc or lacking in background and perspective – attitudes that are common in the private sector, but there the employees have to cope with buzzwords that are less publicly challenged before becoming dogma.

Most importantly, it is difficult to imagine spending billions of dollars without any plan in hand and pursuing goals and guiding people without any sense of direction. Even though head office may sometimes be out of touch with grassroot issues, it will have the final formal word, but the people in the field will have the final real word, since real action is on the field level. The centre will be ultimately held accountable by the political system, which happens to be at the political centre of the country, and through that by all citizens of the country.

Head office has its flaws too. A manager's success is not always what it seems; some public managers, like private colleagues, put their organization in peril just to realize personal success, "not eating the pill completely," as Mintzberg has put it. For instance, listening overly intently to employees may make a manager "a great leader(!)" in his employees' eyes, but this may be done at risk of keeping the organization too inward-looking. Managerial success, in turn, does not always lead to long-term organizational success because of fluctuating local and political expectations in response to changing public-sector policy. Some very successful public-sector executives have been promoted to better positions before the flaws of their policies or management became apparent. Similarly, some private CEOs collected tremendous bonuses for bringing their company to the brink of bankruptcy.

The public sector is so specific that if "managing is managing," its context makes it that the larger part of managerial theory should receive a specific application for public sector. Other aspects simply do not apply, at least for now, although the public sector is evolving and applying to its own context courageous experimentations made in private sector.

There are as many differences in the application of management theory between private and public sectors as there are in different components of public sectors (public, parapublic) and with the different layers of management. The mandate's level of precision and the control exerted by all types of central authorities set them very much apart from their private-sector cousins, as well as from public-agency managers, who would enjoy greater autonomy, would not be publicly accountable and who would work on a very precise mandate. Then the differences with private sector would be according to the product and clientele. All in all, Henry Mintzberg has well illustrated the specifics and challenges of managing publicly.

NOTE

1 I gratefully acknowledge the help of Geoff McIlroy who revised parts of this chapter. All remaining errors are mine.

Contributors

Jacques Bourgault, Professor, Département de Science politique, Université du Québec à Montréal; Associate professor, École nationale d'administration publique

Mohamed Charih, Professor, École nationale d'administration publique

Martine Éthier, Senior Analyst, La Société générale de financement du Québec

Henry Mintzberg, Cleghorn Professor of Management, McGill University

Jennifer Smith, Director, Public Management Research Centre of the Public Policy Forum

Paul G. Thomas, Professor, Department of Political Studies, University of Manitoba

David Zussman, Professor, Faculty of Administration, University of Ottawa; President, Public Policy Forum

MONOGRAPHS ON CANADIAN PUBLIC ADMINISTRATION

MONOGRAPHIES SUR L'ADMINISTRATION PUBLIQUE CANADIENNE

Peter Aucoin, Vincent Lemieux
Co-directeurs / Co-editors

This monograph series is sponsored by the Institute of Public Administration of Canada as part of its continuing endeavour to stimulate and publish writing in the field of Canadian public administration. It is intended to be a complement to other publications sponsored by the Institute such as the Canadian Public Administration Series, the magazine *Public Sector Management*, the journal *Canadian Public Administration* and the Case Program in Canadian Public Administration, as well as the proceedings of its public policy seminars. By launching the monograph series for medium-length manuscripts and those of a more specialized nature, the Institute ensures that there is a wide variety of publication formats for authors in public administration. While the first titles were in the area of urban local government, the series is intended to cover the broad public administration field and is under the guidance of the co-editors and of the Research Committee of the Institute.

Cette collection de monographies est parrainée par l'Institut d'administration publique du Canada et témoigne de l'effort suivi de l'Institut pour promouvoir et publier des écrits dans le domaine de l'administration publique canadienne. Elle a été conçue comme un complément aux autres publications parrainées par l'Institut, telles la Collection administration publique canadienne, le magazine *Management et secteur public*, la revue *Administration publique du Canada* et le Programme de cas en administration publique canadienne, de même que les comptes rendus de ses colloques sur des questions de politique publique. En lançant la collection de monographies pour les ouvrages de longueur moyenne et ceux de nature plus spécialisée, l'Institut s'assure que les auteurs dans le domaine de l'administration publique disposent d'une grande diversité de formats de publications. Bien que les premiers titres traitent du gouvernement local urbain, la collection s'étend à l'ensemble du domaine de l'administration publique et est sous la direction des co-directeurs de même que du Comité de recherche de l'Institut.

Monographs on Canadian Public Administration/
Monographies sur l'administration publique canadienne

1. *Shaping the Canadian City: Essays on Urban Politics and Policy, 1890–1920* – John C. Weaver
2. *Structural Changes in Local Government: Government for Urban Regions* – C.R. Tindal
3. *The Politics of Urban Development: Canadian Urban Expressway Disputes* – Christopher Leo
4. *Quebec's Health System: A Decade of Change, 1967–1977* – Sidney S. Lee
5. *An Approach to Manpower Planning and Management Development in Canadian Municipal Government* – Anne B. McAllister
6. *Le côté humain des systèmes d'information: une vue pratique* – Roland Hurtubise et Pierre Voyer
7. *The Effects of Transition to Confederation on Public Administration in Newfoundland* – J.G. Channing, C.M.
8. *Coordination in Canadian Governments: A Case Study of Aging Policy* – Kenneth Kernaghan and Olivia Kuper
9. *Public Non-Profit Budgeting: The Evolution and Application of Zero-Base Budgeting* – James Cutt and Richard Ritter
10. *Institutions and Influence Groups in Canadian Farm and Food Policy* – J.D. Forbes
11. *Budgeting in the Provinces: Leadership and the Premiers* – Allan M. Maslove (editor)
12. *Getting the Pink Slip: Severances and Firings in the Senior Public Service* – W.A.W. Neilson (editor)
13. *City Management in Canada: The Role of the Chief Administrative Officer (CAO)* – T.J. Plunkett
14. *Taking Power: Managing Government Transitions/Prendre le pouvoir: La gestion des transitions gouvernementales* – Donald J. Savoie (editor / directeur)
15. *Agencies, Boards, and Commissions in Canadian Local Government* – Dale Richmond and David Siegel (editors)
16. *Learning from Others: Administrative Innovations Among Canadian Governments* – James Iain Gow
17. *Hard Choices or No Choices: Assessing Program Review / L'heure des choix difficiles: L'évaluation de l'Examen des programmes* – Amelita Armit and Jacques Bourgault (editors / directeurs)
18. *So-Called Experts: How American Consultants Remade the Canadian Civil Service 1918–21* – Alasdair Roberts
19. *Genesis, Termination and Succession in the Life Cycle of Organizations: The Case of the Maritime Resource Management Service* – M. Paul Brown
20. *New Public Management and Public Administration in Canada/Nouveau management public et administration publique au Canada* – Mohamed Charih and Arthur Daniels (editors/directeurs)
21. *Value for Many: The Institute of Public Administration of Canada, 1947–1997/*